DISCARDED

SEARING INSPIRATION

ALSO BY SUSAN VOLLAND

Mastering Sauces: The Home Cook's Guide
to New Techniques for Fresh Flavors

FAST, ADAPTABLE ENTRÉES AND FRESH PAN SAUCES

SEARING INSPIRATION

SUSAN VOLLAND

PHOTOGRAPHY BY ANGIE NORWOOD BROWNE

FOOD STYLING BY PATTY WITTMANN

W. W. NORTON & COMPANY

Independent Publishers Since 1923

NEW YORK | LONDON

For information about permission to reproduce selections from this book, write to
Permissions, W. W. Norton & Company, Inc., 500 Fifth Avenue, New York, NY 10110

For information about special discounts for bulk purchases, please contact
W. W. Norton Special Sales at specialsales@wwnorton.com or 800-233-4830

Manufacturing by Versa Press
Book design by Level Inc.
Production manager: Anna Oler

Library of Congress Cataloging-in-Publication Data

Names: Volland, Susan, author.
Title: Searing inspiration : fast, adaptable entrées and fresh pan sauces /
   Susan Volland ; photography by Angie Norwood Browne.
Description: First edition. | New York : W. W. Norton & Company, [2018] |
   Includes index.
Identifiers: LCCN 2018028761 | ISBN 9780393292411 (hardcover)
Subjects: LCSH: Skillet cooking. | Sauces. | LCGFT: Cookbooks.
Classification: LCC TX840.S55 V65 2018 | DDC 641.7/7—dc23
LC record available at https://lccn.loc.gov/2018028761

W. W. Norton & Company, Inc., 500 Fifth Avenue, New York, N.Y. 10110
www.wwnorton.com

W. W. Norton & Company Ltd., 15 Carlisle Street, London W1D 3BS

1 2 3 4 5 6 7 8 9 0

FOR SHELLEY, MY SISTER DRAGON

CONTENTS

INTRODUCTION

SEARING FOODS AND MAKING FRESH SAUCES IN A HOT SKILLET CAN BE A GAME changer for busy cooks. It's fast, but there are few, if any, "cheats" or shortcuts. It's "real" cooking, like what you see on a restaurant line. Ingredients aren't just simmered, baked, boiled, or zapped in a microwave. A hot skillet requires continuous interaction. There is sound and steam and, if you feel frisky, maybe even a lick of flame. Chicken, garlic, a splash of wine, and a dollop of butter are simple ingredients, but the finished seared and sauced dish is far from simplistic. The chicken is savory and golden brown but still juicy. The sauce is complex, with depth, aroma, and a touch of brilliance from the slightly acidic wine. A single pat of butter adds silkiness and subtle luxury. It's a meal you want to eat sitting down at the table, with knives and forks, even when it will be only a few minutes before everyone has to start running again.

With every seared and sauced recipe you make, your skills and knowledge grow exponentially. You become more efficient, and it all starts to feel very natural, perhaps even exciting. Pan sauces were traditionally perceived as exclusive, indulgent, and expensive. They were made tableside at fine-dining restaurants. Silky tournedos of beef or tender veal scaloppini were sizzled with shallots, theatrically flambéed with Cognac or a fancy wine, and finished with heaps of cream and butter. Dishes such as these were so artfully prepared that re-creating them at home was hardly even an option. As popular tastes pivoted to fresh, lighter, bolder foods, formal tableside performances were traded in for more exciting open-kitchen floor plans. Pan sauces got more exotic and sometimes even spicy. They were often bound with specialty oils and reductions rather than butter and cream. But the mystique of pan sauces has never waned. Watching a cook skillfully flash-sear and sauté ingredients in a skillet and then, moments later, having a dazzling sauced entrée placed before you is still a culinary magic show.

The speed at which a novice cook can graduate from captive audience member to performer is my favorite part of teaching pan sauces. The skillet, perceived as being perhaps the simplest of all kitchen tools, is utterly exasperating when it doesn't work the way you want it to. Ingredients stick to the pan. Meats weep and simmer rather than brown. A scorched piece of fish or chicken can fill the

> If you think there's a problem, put on the brakes.
> Make adjustments. One of the best things about cooking in a skillet
> is the responsiveness it allows you.

kitchen with smoke and yet still remain raw in the middle. The most common solution? "I need a *good* frying pan." When the food still doesn't improve, another is bought, this time with a magic coating or shocking price tag. I've heard frustrated cooks blame their stoves, insisting that they will only get restaurant-quality results if they have a restaurant-quality range. While I'll never dissuade someone from investing in a good skillet or stove, the tools are rarely the problem. Sure, scratched, wobbly frying pans on teetering, tilted, or clogged burners are not the easiest road to success, but it's knowledge and familiarity with your equipment that really matters. Once you are armed with some simple tips, like how to heat the pan, add the oil to it, and arrange the ingredients in it, foods start to behave. They sizzle and brown, and the kitchen fills with tempting aromas instead of curses.

Watching chefs zoom around a hot line, shooting ingredients into smoking-hot skillets and then flipping and clanging things for a quick minute before everything is plated and whisked to the table can make it seem as if high temperatures and speed equal proficiency. That's not the case. The chefs you are watching have made those dishes hundreds of times. Their prepped ingredients are at their fingertips, and they know exactly which burners are sluggish and which are flame-throwers. They have a dozen things going at once and an audience of hungry diners watching their every move. But yours is not a restaurant kitchen. The first step toward mastering a hot skillet is to slow things down.

First, have a clear idea of what you want and plan how to get there. Take the time to get all your ingredients prepared, measured, and arranged before you step anywhere near the stove. Chefs call this their *mise en place* (see page 27). Instead of cranking the burner to the highest heat, let the pan gradually heat up to the desired temperature. Arrange the food in the skillet deliberately, with care, and then try to leave it alone. Pay attention to sounds and smells, though, as it cooks.

If you think there's a problem, put on the brakes. Make adjustments. One of the best things about cooking in a skillet is the responsiveness it allows you. If a fish fillet doesn't sizzle when you touch it to the oil, pull it out, let the pan heat up some more, and then try again—don't just add another piece of fish to the pan and hope for the best. If, on the other hand, the oil starts smoking the moment you swirl it into the skillet, or the fish spits and crackles, the pan is too hot. Lift it off the burner to cool things down quickly. Rescue those tender fillets before it's too late. If, when you are cooking, the searing is going great but the pan residue starts to blacken, or the minced garlic burns when you start the sauce, *stop!* It's far better to let the seared food sit on a plate for a minute or two while you clean the pan or chop some fresh aromatics than to forge on and then have to choke down an entrée that is infused with those unpleasant flavors. These things happen to everyone, even professionals; pros just fix stuff faster.

I put a lot of emphasis on skillful searing, but my heart is in sauce making. Juicy, well-seared entrées can stand alone, but they are exponentially improved with a drizzle of artful sauce. When you build a pan sauce on a base of a perfect fond, you instantly link the two elements, entrée and finishing sauce, resulting in not just another piece of meat or chicken on the plate, but a unified, complex dish. Seared chicken adds an essence of chicken flavor to the sauce. If you substitute salmon fillets or shrimp, the sauce will have a nuance of seafood. The savory juices that were released during the cooking process are recaptured and reintroduced into the final preparation. Just don't expect a fantastic pan sauce to camouflage a poorly cooked or less-than-fresh main ingredient, and remember that few things can cheapen a prime steak faster than a glop of lazy sauce.

My hope is that by reading this book, you will become more comfortable with your ingredients and tools, will cook with more spontaneity, and, eventually, will trust your own taste and instincts enough to create unique dishes with ingredients on hand rather than be strictly bound to written recipes. At the market, instead of leaning on your shopping cart, staring blankly at the displays and awaiting dinner inspiration, you will search out the freshest items and best deals. And, like me, you will keep your kitchen stocked with staples such as fresh garlic, shallot, wines, and herbs, with a stash of chicken, shrimp, and steaks in the freezer. So, when you get home from the market, you can turn on the music, and maybe sip some wine, while you "throw something together." And you'll still have time to make that parent-teacher meeting or evening class, or even enjoy some well-deserved couch contact. The pizza guy will just have to manage without you.

HOW TO USE THIS BOOK

The focus of this book is on techniques, not just recipes. Many of these dishes rely on the same techniques of searing, deglazing, and embellishing, even when the ingredients are very different. Once you understand these fundamentals, you should be able to adapt and customize these and other recipes to suit your tastes. There are also a few recipes here that veer from the basic formula to illustrate how diverse pan sauces can be: Gravies, for example, are made by starting with a roux rather than a deglazing liquid, while other sauces are based on purees, vinaigrettes, or even emulsified egg yolks. Follow the recipes as written until you have a clear understanding of what happens at each step, then cut loose and have some fun.

Each Recipe Suggests Alternatives to the Main Ingredient.

The heading "*This Sauce Also Goes Well with . . .*" is followed by a short list of other main ingredients that also pair well with the flavor profile of the sauce. The Warm Salsa Criolla (page 168), for example, is delicious on mild-flavored fish, although the original recipe calls for calf's liver. I didn't suggest steak as one of the recommended alternatives for the Fennel and Grapefruit Beurre Blanc (page 56), because beef would overpower the delicate floral flavors of the sauce. I came up with these pairings during the testing process, although I haven't tried them all yet. My selections were chosen first for flavor and texture, then techniques, and then adaptability for varied diets. I tried to limit the number to four or five even where there may be dozens of good alternatives.

Mix and Match the SEAR and SAUCE.

For inspiration, try switching the recipe titles around. Putting emphasis on the sauce rather than the main ingredient can make it easier to see potential in other more familiar or accessible alternatives. Recasting the recipe for Flatiron Steak with Warm Green Vinaigrette as "Warm Green Vinaigrette on Flatiron Steak" takes the focus away from the specialty cut, so you can see now how easy it would be to substitute a sirloin or rib-steak,

or maybe even chicken, kielbasa, or shrimp. The Sauce Index (pages 227–29) removes the main ingredients from the titles altogether. Vegetarians and pescatarians can land on the Bell Pepper Relish (page 158) even if the Italian sausages in the original recipe aren't their thing. I have also incorporated a clear demarcation between the prep, searing, and sauce-making steps of a recipe to make mixing and matching easier.

Adjust the Serving Sizes to Suit Your Needs.

My recipes usually include a weight range for the main ingredient that will fit in a large skillet and a variance in the yield that is dependent on who's at the dinner table. Scaling a recipe down rather than up tends to be more successful. If you worry that the portions are small, you want to add more meat, fish, or chicken, but do not over-

crowd the pan. Keep in mind that when you make changes such as these, the ratio of sauce to main ingredient will be altered. If you cook 2 mushroom caps instead of the 4 called for in the recipe, you will end up with extra sauce—but I've yet to have anyone complain that there was too much of that good sauce.

First Focus on the Main Ingredient, Then Build the Sauce. Marry the Two Before Serving.

Split Cornish game hens may taste like chicken, but they cook very differently from thin boneless chicken breast cutlets. Seared eggplant will not leave the savory brown residue of a pork chop in the pan. Ingredients of a similar size, density, and thickness are the

easiest trades; for instance, boneless chicken thighs can easily be swapped for boneless chicken breasts. If you aren't sure how to adapt a recipe, refer to the tables on pages 208–26 in the "Improvising" chapter for guidance. My assumption is that you know not to serve chicken drumsticks medium-rare, even if the original recipe for strip steak suggests that doneness.

I have done my best to offer visual clues and reference points, not just times, in the recipes. Please use these—and some common sense—when you are swapping out main ingredients. A really thick chunk of halibut might call for 4 minutes of searing and then another 4 minutes of pan-roasting until "the flakes are loose but the fish is still slightly translucent at the thickest point." Thin sole fillets, though, which are also best cooked to that point, take a fraction of time, maybe 2 minutes total. Don't continue to cook the sole as if it were halibut! Move on to the next step. If you aren't sure, refer again to the "Improvising" chapter, as well as to the safe-temperatures recommendations on page 17.

Then make your sauces with a similar approach. Follow the visual clues, such as reducing it until it clings to a spoon or becomes syrupy. But since timing will change with the alternative ingredients suggested, you may need to add a splash more liquid if things seem dry, or to continue to simmer the sauce if it needs more thickening or concentration. Take control of the texture of your sauces—that is one of my three fundamentals of sauce making (see page 15).

Finally, marry the sauce and the main ingredient before you serve the dish. That may mean simmering the seared food in the sauce for a minute, or draping "just enough" sauce over the plated entrée so that it doesn't seem smothered and serving the rest alongside, or perhaps drizzling a dish with top-notch oil or a fresh garnish to pull the elements together.

Be Prepared for the Occasional Disaster.

Let me take a moment to assure you that you're going to have some disasters. That's the reality of cooking, and it's particularly true when you start experimenting. Not every attempt at fine art produces a masterwork. Michelangelo and Stravinsky had bad days. So, perhaps save the best Italian marble until you see your David. Don't buy the Stradi-varius before you've mastered your scales. In other words, save buying those expensive, boutique duck breasts for when you've got chicken figured out. And don't expect a spontaneous concoction of almond butter, pickle juice, and feta cheese to be the sauce of your dreams.

MY THREE FUNDAMENTALS OF SAUCE MAKING

I believe there are three fundamentals behind good sauce making: Maximize Flavor, Manipulate Texture, and Season Confidently. When you keep your focus on these core principles, you assume control of your ingredients and recipes. Most sauce-making lessons start with classic bases that are then adapted to suit various preparations. I prefer to make independent choices at every step, from ingredient selection to final flourish. I say it all the time: "The *right* way to make a sauce is *your* way." My three sauce-making fundamentals are discussed in depth in my first book, *Mastering Sauces*, but here are some key points you should keep in mind.

1. MAXIMIZE FLAVOR

Start with good ingredients and do your best to keep them that way.

Consider every drop of liquid you incorporate, because once these are in there, you can't pick them out. Is your fresh lemon juice sweet and aromatic, or sharp and watery? Is the stock salty? Does it have a strong onion flavor? Be continually aware of how each ingredient will affect the finished product.

You aren't going to get a good sauce if you start with bad wine.

Treat oils like precious ingredients. Most flavors are oil-soluble, so when fats are dispersed throughout a dish, more flavors are made accessible. Use fresh, good-quality fats and take care of them (e.g., be careful not to burn the butter). Discard any oil that has become spent and overheated during the cooking process. Feature your best oils by drizzling them over a finished dish rather than burying them in a pungent dressing or cooking away their attributes. Again, if you start your sauce by infusing old oil with burnt garlic, every drop of sauce will carry that unpleasant infusion.

2. MANIPULATE TEXTURE

Always remember that *you* have control of the texture of your sauce. Adjustments might include simmering or reducing, adding a thickener, straining, pureeing, or changing the temperature of the sauce.

3. SEASON CONFIDENTLY

Taste consciously. "Feel" how the sauce stimulates your palate and make adjustments as needed with elements that are salty, sweet, sour, bitter, or savory (i.e., umami)

Make sure it tastes good to you. Taste is personal and unique. When you season your sauces to suit your tastes, you know that at least one person at the table will be satisfied.

RECIPE SPECIFICS

Start with fresh, good-quality ingredients. Chop your own garlic, squeeze your own lemons, and use fresh herbs. Look for specialty items at international markets and gourmet shops, or order them online.

Ingredients vary regionally. The fish fillets, meat cuts, chicken breasts, and apples you buy, for example, may very well be different from mine. I have done my best to work to a common standard and to offer alternatives when appropriate.

"Peeled" is implied for ingredients like onions, garlic, shallots, carrots, and ginger.

FOOD SAFETY

Educate yourself on the basics of safe food handling. Use only ingredients that have been well sourced. Keep your work surfaces and tools clean and be vigilant about the possibility of cross-contamination.

Never underestimate the severity of food allergies.

Invest in a good-quality instant-read thermometer (see page 21). If you or someone you are cooking for has medical concerns or a compromised immune system, never take risks or serve foods like raw or undercooked eggs, poultry, meat, or fish. Some chefs choose to serve foods at temperatures they feel best showcase the ingredients. For example, I like duck breast served medium-rare—That can increase the risk of food-borne illness. All decisions about internal cooking temperature, and any potential risks, are ultimately your own.

TEMPERATURE RECOMMENDATIONS

	CHEF RECOMMENDATIONS	USDA RECOMMENDATIONS
BEEF AND LAMB		
Standard recommendation for all		145°F/63°C
Ground Meats	160°F/71°C	160°F/71°C
Bleu/Blue	110°F/43°C	
Rare	120° to 130°F/49° to 54°C	
Medium-Rare	130° to 135°F/54° to 57°C	
Medium	135° to 145°F/57° to 63°C	
Medium-Well	145° to 155°F/63° to 68°C	
Well	155°F+/68°C+	
Organ Meats	Varies	160° to 170°F/71° to 76°C
PORK		
Standard recommendation for all		145°F/63°C
Sausage	160°F/71°C	160°F/71°C
Medium	137°F/58°C	
Well	145°F/63°C	145°F/63°C
Precooked Ham and Cured Meats	120°F/49°C	140° to 165°F/60° to 74°C
POULTRY		
Standard recommendation for all		165°F/74°C
Whole or Ground	165°F/74°C	165°F/74°C
Legs and Thighs	170° to 180°F/77° to 82°C	
Duck Breast	130° to 140°F/54° to 60°C	160° to 170°F/71° to 76°C
FISH AND SEAFOOD		
Standard recommendation for all		145°F/63°C
Sashimi-Grade Tuna	115°F/46°C	
Shrimp	120°F/49°C	
Salmon	125°F/52°C	
Halibut	130°F/54°C	
Scallops	130°F/54°C	
Lobster	140°F/60°C	

Tools for searing: slotted spatulas, instant-read thermometer, tongs, towels, pepper mill, knives

TOOLS AND EQUIPMENT

I t's the cook, not the equipment, that makes a great meal. If you have tools that please you, keep using them. If they frustrate you, or you have started to recognize their limitations, it's time to go shopping.

ASSORTED 10- AND 12-INCH SKILLETS

A 12-inch skillet is the most commonly used tool in this book. There are a few recipes that fit tidily in a smaller pan, and if you regularly cook for 1 or 2 people, a 10- or even 8-inch skillet may be preferable. My current favorites are All-Clad stainless steel, classic cast iron, and well-seasoned carbon steel. I avoid nonstick skillets and "cheater" pans—those that are flared to 12 inches at the top but actually have a much smaller cooking surface.

While researching this book, I started obsessing about core metals measured in fractions of millimeters and international cladding standards. When cast-iron pore size and anodizing techniques started to seem like important life decisions, I knew it was time to step away from the computer. We're talking about dinner here, not space travel. I'm not saying that composition and manufacturing don't matter, but if your chicken piccata burns, it's not because the copper layer in your skillet is a micron too thin.

4- OR 5-QUART LIDDED SAUTÉ PAN

"Sauté pan" is currently the accepted term for a large skillet with straight, not sloping, sides and a lid. A whole chicken cut into 8 pieces fits snugly in a 5-quart sauté pan. To me, that seems like reason enough to buy one. You can sear, sauté, and even roast, braise, and stew in these pans. But the large amount of surface area can be too much when searing smaller items or quantities, so they shouldn't be considered a one-size-fits-all tool.

> ## AVOID NONSTICK PANS
> Pan sauces are best when they are built on the flavorful residue and sticky bits that cling to the bottom of a skillet. You don't get those in nonstick skillets. And when you use good searing techniques and a good-quality skillet, sticking is rarely a problem.

REMOVABLE SILICONE PAN HANDLES

Some really good pans have horrifically uncomfortable handles; carbon-steel skillets can be particularly bad. But for around ten bucks, you can remedy that by sliding on a comfortable silicone sleeve. These are heatproof, so they can go into a moderate oven. There are various brands, colors, and sizes.

Shop around to make sure what you select works with the tools you have.

UNIVERSAL LIDS

A universal lid is a flat disk with a handle that can be used to cover pots and pans of various sizes. Skillets are rarely sold with lids, but sometimes it is helpful to halt the evaporation of a sauce or capture steam to cook the main ingredients through. A universal lid means that you don't have to hunt around for something that fits.

KNIVES

Invest in good, well-balanced knives. Keep them sharp, clean them immediately, and never put them in the dishwasher or sink. This is kitchen gospel; you will never meet a chef who disagrees. An 8- to 10-inch French chef's knife and a few good paring knives may be the most important tools in my kitchen. A santoku knife is a traditional Japanese knife with a boxier, more-squared shape and "hollow blade" grooves to prevent vegetables and other ingredients from sticking to it. It has become standard equipment for many chefs these days, but I've never developed a feel for one. Other recommendations include a Chinese cleaver; a tapered round-tipped meat-cutting knife; a fillet knife; and a good serrated bread knife. A carving knife and fork and good set of steak knives are also nice.

POULTRY SHEARS

I have never once regretted buying my Wüsthof-Trident poultry shears. When I was a young line cook, the price tag initially made me gasp, but these are absolutely the perfect tool for breaking down a whole chicken, splitting game hens, and trimming fish. I've tried cheaper models, but they don't compare.

CUTTING BOARDS

Cutting boards need to rest solidly on the counter, with no bouncing or sliding. Good large cutting boards can reduce prep time. Small cutting boards that become crowded are unsafe because foods can roll under the knife. I suggest having both wood and polyethylene boards in a few sizes. Some cooks like to use color-coded boards to signify which are used for raw meats and which for vegetables. These are handy, but awareness of cross-contamination hazards and good food handling habits are even more effective at preventing illness.

CARVING BOARD

A carving board is a wooden cutting board with a shallow trough around the perimeter for capturing meat juices. I almost always slice steaks before serving them. Resting steaks before slicing them will greatly reduce the flow of juices, but with a carving board, the juices that do run stay on the board rather than flow onto the countertop.

MEAT POUNDER OR SMOOTH MALLET

Cutlets and scaloppini have to be pounded flat, and for that, you need a smooth meat pounder or mallet. It should be metal so it can be thoroughly cleaned. Don't use mallets with sharp edges or a waffled surface to pound cutlets—those are for tenderizing, not flattening. I use an inexpensive aluminum mallet that stands in my utensil jar alongside the whisks and tongs.

TONGS

My spring-loaded tongs are almost an extension of my hands. I can hardly cook without them. Tongs should be sturdy, with no sharp edges, and a good weight and balance. The spring should be easy to clamp but quick to open.

SPATULAS

Slotted offset fish spatulas, sometimes known as Peltex spatulas, have a long, thin, angled blade that can easily slide between the food and the pan. Tender fillets of fish can be flipped or lifted out of the pan with less risk of them breaking. The slotted surface means foods can be lifted out of a liquid so the sauce remains in the pan. If you are left-handed, make sure you buy one that is tapered in the correct direction.

Flexible silicone spatulas are helpful for stirring sauces and squeegeeing every last drop from the skillet. A good pancake flipper is also handy.

WOODEN SPOONS

Few tools are better for loosening the sticky brown bits at the bottom of a pan than a wooden spoon. It can be used quite aggressively, with no risk of the sauce picking up the faint metallic taste or gray color that can come from scraping metal on metal. Wooden spoons with flat edges work particularly well in skillets. (If there are "lefties" in your house, make sure you have spoons that taper both to the left and the right.) More and more craftspeople are selling handmade wooden spoons. They are beautiful and durable, and, as I have learned from experience, they make excellent travel souvenirs.

INSTANT-READ THERMOMETERS

Thermometers take the guesswork out of cooking meat and poultry. I have half a dozen types, but I've found that the cheaper ones need regular calibrating: Test them often in boiling water or ice water. I love the ThermoWorks Thermapen. The tip is both fine and sensitive, so I can take a reading quickly without poking a big hole in my food.

SMALL WHISKS

Big balloon-shaped whisks are designed to create and incorporate air bubbles. Elongated narrow whisks efficiently blend sauce ingredients without making them fluffy or foamy; they are particularly useful for finishing sauces made with cold butter. My favorite is an 8-inch model made by Best Manufacturers. I've had it for decades.

MEASURING TOOLS

Make sure you have both dry and liquid measuring cups, as well as measuring spoons. I was given a few small liquid measures, kind of like oversized shot glasses with volume marks, and they are great for making pan sauces. I can pour a measured amount of vinegar or sherry without reaching for the spoons or cup measures.

Assorted oils: peanut, toasted sesame,
extra virgin olive, "neutral" safflower

WIDE TWEEZERS
OR NEEDLE-NOSE PLIERS

Salmon bones can easily be pulled from fillets with a good pair of tweezers with flat, wide tips or clean needle-nose pliers.

SMALL PREP DISHES AND BOWLS

Everything should be measured, chopped, minced, or otherwise prepped before you step up to the stove. Small dishes make assembling your *mise en place* much easier.

OIL BOTTLES

I have two clear plastic squeeze bottles I keep next to the stove. One holds a neutral vegetable oil and the other peanut oil. When I can squeeze a thin stream or a few drops exactly where I want, I use less oil. There are fancy oil carafes if you want something a bit prettier. Or you might use the "speed pour" tops that fit into bottle tops like corks so you can keep good olive oil or unrefined oils in their original dark bottles. But keep just enough oil in these bottles to use for a few weeks and store the rest in a dark, cool place.

TASTING SPOONS

When you have lots of spoons within easy reach, you are much more likely to taste your food as it cooks. I bought a stack of cheap small spoons at a restaurant supply store and keep them in a cup near the stovetop so I don't have to pull spoons from my table setting.

GLASS PIE PLATES, PLAIN OVAL
PLATTERS, AND SIMILAR LARGE,
SHALLOW DISHES

You never realize how much you take your own equipment for granted until you work in someone else's kitchen. I now see how hopelessly dependent I am on my glass pie plates and oval platters. The pie plates are perfect for holding meats while you prep the other ingredients, for dredging, and for ferrying main ingredients from the cutting board to the skillet. I am always pleased with the way seared and sauced items look on plain glass or white ceramic platters.

PARCHMENT PAPER

I like to cover pieces of meat and poultry with parchment paper before pounding them into cutlets or scaloppini. The paper helps give me a feel for the resistance and pressure that is needed. If the paper tears, I am pounding too hard. Squares or strips of parchment are also excellent for separating stacked individual patties, cutlets, or fillets so they don't stick together.

THE BASICS

Mise en place for Spiced Coconut Oil
(page 61): (clockwise from bottom)
turmeric, powdered chile, ginger, fresh
curry leaves, black mustard seeds,
sliced shallots, cumin seeds

Mise en Place:
Have Everything Ready Before You Start

Mise en place is a French phrase that means "everything in place." To assemble your *mise* is to have your tools gathered and your ingredients cut, measured, and ready to go before you step up to the stove. It's a great habit to get into. It can take as little as two minutes to flash-sear a thin steak to medium-rare. You don't want to set that sizzling steak aside while you mince an onion or try to find the cumin.

Cooking Oil:
Neutral Oils, Clarified Butter, and Specialty Oils

Many of the recipes in this book call for "neutral oil." Neutral oils are light in flavor, color, and aroma. Calling for neutral oil in a recipe gets around the clumsiness of calling for "2 tablespoons canola, safflower, soy, or vegetable oil" and inevitably omitting several other good mild-flavored options. A friend once asked me, "Why don't you just say canola oil? Everyone is going to use canola anyway, right?" Personally, I don't cook with canola because I don't like the smell. My neutral oils of choice are safflower, rice bran, and raw sesame oil.

Clarified butter is pure butterfat. Ghee is also clarified butter. The milk solids have been removed, so the butter can reach searing temperatures without burning. Foods fried in clarified butter can have more flavor than foods cooked in neutral oil.

To make clarified butter, melt a stick or two of unsalted butter in a small saucepan and bring to a full boil. Remove the pan from the heat and let the melted butter cool and settle for 10 minutes. Skim off any scum from the top and decant the clear butterfat, leaving the cloudy milk solids behind.

I sometimes call for peanut or olive oil. Peanut oil has a high temperature threshold, and it is my favorite frying oil for stir-frying and for many Asian-inspired dishes. Olive oil is a kitchen staple in most households. Some cooks use extra-virgin olive oil for everything, but I rarely do. The better the olive oil, the less heat-tolerant it is. Save your best oils for drizzling over finished dishes.

What Is Searing?

To sear is to brown, char, or darken with high heat. It is a surface treatment. It can be done in a skillet, on a hot grill, or under a broiler. Many braised, stewed, simmered, and even roasted foods are seared first for added color and flavor. Sautéed and stir-fried ingredients can pick up a nice brown sear in a hot pan. Some may argue that searing food in a pan is just a prettied-up description of frying, but it is best done with just a thin film of oil and minimal agitation.

Always Heat the Empty Skillet First and Then Add the Oil

Train yourself to never put food in a cold skillet. Heat the pan to your ideal cooking temperature, swirl in a little oil, and then add the food. That way, the ingredients start to cook at the right temperature immediately. You would never put a cake in a cold oven or steaks on a lukewarm grill—why put ingredients in a cool skillet? Check the surface temperature by splashing in about ⅛ teaspoon water: It will bead up and skitter at a good searing temperature. If the water bubbles and steams, the pan isn't hot enough. If it crackles, spits, and disappears instantly, the pan is too hot. Preheating your pan also prevents sticking. A sheen of oil in a hot pan creates its own nonstick surface. Ingredients almost hydroplane over the hot metal.

Arrange the Ingredients in the Pan Deliberately

The more care you take in placing food in the skillet, the better the food will cook and look. Add the pieces gradually, and leave space between them. The last item, not just the first, should sizzle. It's better to sear foods in batches than to overload the pan.

THE "PRESENTATION SIDE"

The first surface of the food to contact the pan will always have a better color and more even sear. After you flip the food, the surface will never be as pristine. So, before you start cooking, look at your ingredients and decide which side you want to serve "up." That is the presentation side, and it should contact the pan surface first. If you are cooking items like lamb chops or shrimp, arrange them in the pan all facing the same direction; when cooked, they will look nicer on the plate or platter.

Listen!

A good sear always starts with a sizzle. It is the sound of fat and water interacting in a sort of land battle. If the oil expels the water, the temperature can rise high enough to start the Maillard reaction and the food will start to brown. If the water wins, the foods will start to steam and simmer and the temperature cannot increase until the water has boiled away. Patting foods dry and not overcrowding the pan help ensure a proper sizzle and sear. Touch one of the ingredients to the pan. If there is silence, let the pan heat a bit longer. If it crackles loudly or spits, remove the skillet from the heat for a few seconds to cool it slightly.

What If It Sticks?

When you preheat your pan, swirl in the oil and then place your food carefully, you have greatly reduced the chance of sticking. Many ingredients will still cling to the pan at first, but they will eventually release cleanly if you leave them alone. Let me say it again—if it sticks, leave it alone! As the food continues to brown and firm up, the molecular bond formed between the soft proteins and microscopic divots in the pan starts to loosen. Items that seem hopelessly stuck will usually release with a gentle nudge or light tug if you let them cook a bit longer. Rigorous pulling or scraping before meats are well seared will tear them. Soft foods can end up looking particularly mangled.

Pan-Roasting and Other Secondary Cooking Techniques

Searing is a surface treatment. Some ingredients, like sole fillets and thin scaloppini, may be nearly cooked through by the time they turn brown, but thick steaks and poultry with bones require more time. You can reduce the heat and regularly flip the items until they reach your preferred internal temperature, or you can use a secondary cooking technique, like simmering or steaming.

I like to pan-roast seared items. It helps maintain a dry surface and crisp brown crust while avoiding the fiddle of constantly flipping slower-cooking foods on the stovetop. To pan-roast, heat the oven to a moderately high temperature, like 425° to 450°F/220° to 230°C before you start to cook. Sear the first side of the ingredients to a proper brown as usual, then flip the pieces and pop the skillet into the oven. The hot pan surface will continue to brown the second side by conduction, but everything will also be heated by convection. Foods will cook through more quickly and evenly than with direct heat alone.

Continue to monitor the progress closely; setting a timer for regular check-ins is recommended—when items are no longer in your line of vision, they can easily be forgotten.

The Magic of "Fond": Treasure the Brown, Sticky Residue

The sticky brown bits that collect on the bottom of a pan when you sear food are so important to pan sauces and gravies that they have a fancy French name, *fond*, which means foundation. This blend of concentrated juices, fats, and crispy scraps adds unmatched savory flavor and color to stocks, broths, soups, and sauces. Treasure it. When you build a sauce from a fond, you are able to marry the sauce and the seared elements into a more cohesive, complex, and richly flavored dish.

Meats make the darkest fonds. Lean seafood, vegetables, and soy products don't leave much, if any, fond. But bright flavor-packed sauces can be made in residue-free pans, so don't stress if you are starting your sauce in an essentially clean pan.

Discard the Spent Frying Oil and Any Unappealing Bits

I almost always pour out the spent, overheated cooking oil and start with fresh oil or butter before sautéing or softening additional ingredients. One of my sauce-making fundamentals is that oils should be treated like precious materials. Fats carry flavors even better than waters. Do you really want every drop of sauce to taste of burnt, acrid-smelling oil? But animal fats, like those rendered from bacon or pancetta, poultry, or ground meats, tend to maintain their flavor even after they are cooked to the smoke point, so they can be salvaged.

After searing the food, inspect what remains in the skillet. The fond should be sticky and brown, not black and flaky. A great pan sauce cannot be created from a base of burnt residue or scorched dredging flour. If that is what you see and smell, clean the pan before continuing.

Small bits of meat or seafood are often left in a pan after searing. Sometimes these

Enriching a pan sauce with butter (see page 32).

can soften up and add flavor to a sauce, or melt into relative invisibility in the sauce. But if you think the tidbits look burnt or unattractive, scoop them out. A quick wipe with a paper towel should swipe away unwelcome particles without dislodging a good fond.

Don't Burn the Aromatics

When you sauté aromatic ingredients like minced shallots, leeks, or garlic in the pan before you deglaze it, the resulting sauce will have more depth, pungency, and complex flavor. These minced bits, though, especially garlic, will burn quickly at searing temperatures, and that bitterness will be infused into every drop of sauce. So in these recipes, I often suggest cooling the skillet slightly before adding fresh oil and aromatics. If you do take them a bit too far, it's best to wipe out the pan with a paper towel and start again.

Deglazing

To deglaze a pan is to swish some liquid into it and rehydrate the fond. Water works. Wine is better. Wine or spirits should be simmered at least until the "raw" smell of the alcohol is cooked off. A concentrated, seasoned deglazing liquid is the simplest of all pan sauces.

Finishing Sauces with Butter or Cream

Pan sauces are famously enriched with butter or cream. To finish a sauce with butter, cut up the butter and drop it a few pieces at a time into the simmering sauce. Shake the pan or stir until the butter just liquefies and gently thickens the sauce. For most pan sauces, 1 to 2 tablespoons of butter is plenty. Butter-enriched sauces don't hold particularly well—they congeal when they get cold and can "break" and look greasy if they are overcooked. Heavy cream and crème fraîche can be stirred into hot sauces, but sour cream, light cream, and yogurt must be tempered with a bit of the warm sauce before they are added, or they can "shatter" into tiny beads.

Always Taste and
Adjust the Seasonings before Serving

Season the main ingredient before it is seared. Season the sauce lightly as you make it. And *always* taste your food and make adjustments before you serve it. Both the main ingredient and the sauce should be so well made that that they could stand alone. Don't expect one to carry the other.

Tips for Making Your Seared and Sauced Dishes
Look Their Best

Plate and garnish foods right before serving so they remain vibrant.

Serve sauces at the right temperature. Warm your plates slightly to prevent sauces from congealing or cooling too quickly.

Consider slicing thicker cuts of meat before you serve them. Slicing on a bias can make the pieces look bigger and lie flatter.

Moisten the food with sauce, but don't smother it. Serve any extra sauce alongside.

Try to make your plates have life and movement. Items should be neither too crowded nor isolated. It's nice when they touch here and there. Don't press things down or smooth them out. Use your sauce to lead the eye and connect the elements.

Wipe splatters, smears, and fingerprints from the plate rims before serving.

Making It a Meal

Seared and sauced entrées are excellent centerpieces, and simple dishes can be the best accompaniments: steamed seasonal vegetables, salads, even just sliced tomatoes or fresh fruit. Unassuming grains, potatoes, or beans are often more appropriate than a rich, labor-intensive risotto or pasta. Or choose sides that can hold, like pilafs, gratins, or dressed vegetables and salads. That gives you the time (and space) to focus on searing, saucing, and serving your entrée. And bread is always good for sopping up last drops.

When you are assembling your mise en place, make mental notes of points in the recipes where things might be stopped or held. Also check for last-minute details, like a garnish of grated cheese or chopped fresh herbs.

FISH AND SEAFOOD

Classic Sole Meunière

It's hard to improve on the perfect simplicity of sole meunière. Flash-cooked tender fillets are topped with nothing more than browned butter, a squeeze of lemon, and a sprinkling of parsley. I like to get the fish from the skillet onto the plate as quickly as possible, so I rarely make more than 2 portions.

Pick out fillets that are evenly sized. If the tail ends of the fillets seem paper-thin, consider folding them under to even out the thickness and cooking time. If you don't like the dark brown flecks of brown butter, fry the fish in clarified butter or ghee.

THIS SAUCE ALSO GOES WELL WITH: trout, snapper, calamari steaks, and chicken or veal scaloppini (refer to the tables on pages 208–26 for cooking tips).

YIELD: 2 SERVINGS

8 to 10 ounces (225 to
   285 g) sole fillets
Salt and very finely ground
   white pepper
2 to 3 tablespoons all-purpose
   flour for dredging
3 tablespoons unsalted butter
2 tablespoons freshly
   squeezed lemon juice
1 tablespoon finely chopped
   fresh parsley

PREP

Pat the fish fillets dry and season with salt and white pepper. (If you don't have white pepper, it is better to omit the pepper than to cover the fish with specks of black pepper.) Dredge the sole in the flour and pat off any excess.

SEAR

Heat a large skillet over medium-high heat. When it is hot, add 2 tablespoons of the butter and heat until foamy. Arrange the fillets in the pan so they are evenly spaced. They should sizzle the moment they touch the hot butter. (If there is not enough room in the pan for all of the fish, cook it in batches, wiping the pan clean and starting with fresh butter as needed.) Cook the sole until it is golden brown on the first side, then carefully flip with a long spatula and cook on the other side until the fish just starts to flake at the thickest point. Thin sole fillets may take only 2 minutes; thicker fillets may take 3 or 4. The fish will continue to cook slightly as it rests. Remove the skillet from the heat and lift the sole onto a serving platter or plates.

SAUCE

Analyze the pan residue and remove any unappealing bits. Add the remaining tablespoon of butter to the hot pan. When it is melted, stir in the lemon juice and parsley and use a wooden spoon to dissolve any brown residue in the pan.

Pour the sauce over the fish. Season the dish with a small sprinkle of additional salt. Serve immediately.

DREDGING

A thin coating of flour helps protect wet or tender foods from the high heat of searing. To dredge an ingredient, place a few tablespoons of all-purpose flour, rice flour, or other fine particulate on a plate or shallow dish. It takes less than ¼ cup to coat 4 average-sized chicken cutlets or fish fillets. Nestle a piece of well-seasoned food into the flour, sprinkle some of the flour over the top, and then flip and repeat. I was taught to use only one hand when coating foods. The other should remain clean "in case the phone rings." Inspect the item to double check it is fully coated, then give it a shake and pat lightly to remove all but a powder-fine layer. Excess flour just falls off and will burn in the hot pan.

Coating items in crusts, crumbs, breading, or batter are also excellent surface treatments for pan-fried foods, but the more coating there is, the less fond remains in the pan, so I have chosen to omit them in this book.

Salmon with Buttery French Pea and Lettuce Broth

This is an early spring dish, perfect for when wild salmon start to run and peas are at their sweetest. It was inspired by a classic French preparation of tender greens and peas in a buttery, wine-laced broth. The salmon is first seared and then simmered to perfection in a flavorful pan sauce/broth. The sauce is part delicate broth and part rich beurre blanc. You can add sliced blanched asparagus to the peas and stir in a touch of cream or crème fraîche with the butter if you like.

💡 **THIS SAUCE ALSO GOES WELL WITH:** Arctic char, black cod, snapper, chicken breast "tenders," and split lobster tails (refer to the tables on pages 208–26 for cooking tips).

YIELD: 2 LARGE OR 4 MODERATE SERVINGS

1 to 1½ pounds (450 to 675 g) wild salmon fillet(s)

Salt and finely ground white pepper

2 to 3 tablespoons all-purpose flour for dredging

1 tablespoon clarified butter, light olive oil, or neutral oil

2 tablespoons minced shallots

⅓ cup dry white wine, such as Sauvignon Blanc or Pinot Gris, or extra-dry vermouth

⅔ cup fish stock or low-sodium chicken stock

½ cup green peas (fresh or frozen)

2 cups loosely packed chopped Bibb lettuce

> continues on next page

PREP

Rub your hand gently along the top of the salmon to check for bones. If any remain, pull them out with tweezers. The fish can be cut into individual fillets or left whole and served family-style, if it fits in the skillet. Pat the salmon dry and season generously with salt and white pepper. (Black pepper will leave specks that are unappealing in this dish.) Dredge the fish in the flour and pat off the excess.

SEAR

Heat a lidded sauté pan over medium-high heat. When it is hot, swirl in just enough butter to coat the bottom. Arrange the fish in the pan; if the fillet has been cut into pieces, make sure they are evenly spaced. The fish should sizzle the moment it hits the hot surface. (If there is not enough room in the pan for all of the pieces, cook them in batches, wiping the pan clean and starting with fresh butter as needed.) Sear until the salmon is golden brown on the first side, about 3 minutes. Lift the fish from the pan and place it browned side up on a clean plate or platter. (It will not be cooked through at this point.)

> continues on next page

1 tablespoon minced fresh
   tender herbs, such as chives,
   tarragon, dill, and/or chervil
2 tablespoons cold unsalted
   butter, cut into pats or small cubes
Thinly sliced radishes for
   garnish (optional)

SAUCE

Discard the cooking fat and analyze the pan residue. Remove any unappealing bits. Cool the pan slightly, then return it to medium heat. Add some more butter if the pan is very dry. Add the shallots and sauté until they have softened but not browned, about 1 minute. Deglaze the pan with the wine and use a wooden spoon to dissolve any residue on the bottom of the pan. Increase the heat slightly and simmer until the aroma of raw alcohol is gone and the volume is reduced by half.

Return the fish and any accumulated juices to the skillet and add the stock. Cover and simmer gently until the fish is just cooked through; it should start to flake but still be slightly translucent in the center. Fillets that are 1 inch/2.5 cm thick should take only 3 to 4 minutes; thicker fillets will take a bit longer. The fish will continue to cook slightly as it rests. Lift the fish from the cooking liquid and arrange on a serving platter that will hold a thin, brothy sauce or in shallow bowls.

Simmer the cooking liquid for a minute longer to concentrate the flavors slightly. Add the peas. If you are using fresh peas, they will need about 2 minutes to cook through; if you are using frozen peas, heat them only long enough to take the chill off. Add the chopped lettuce and herbs and stir until the lettuce has just wilted, about 30 seconds. Be careful not to overcook it; the lettuce will continue to soften in the warm sauce. Stir in the butter a few pieces at a time until just liquefied; do not boil the sauce after the butter has been added. Taste and adjust the seasoning with additional salt and pepper as needed.

Spoon the vegetables and sauce over the fish, garnish with the radishes, and serve immediately.

Salmon with Buttery French Pea and Lettuce Broth (page 39)

Salmon with Tomato, Fennel, and Saffron Oil

My favorite way to cook salmon in a skillet is to pan-roast it after the initial searing. It cooks more quickly and evenly that way, and there is less lingering aroma in the kitchen. This olive oil–based sauce was inspired by the flavors of one of my all-time favorite dishes, bouillabaisse, the saffron-laced simmered seafood stew from Marseilles.

THIS SAUCE ALSO GOES WELL WITH: fresh sardines, swordfish steaks, split lobster tails, chicken, and lamb chops (refer to the tables on pages 208–26 for cooking tips).

YIELD: 2 LARGE OR 4 MODERATE SERVINGS

1 medium pinch (about ⅛ teaspoon) saffron threads
1 tablespoon warm water
1 to 1½ pounds (450 to 675 g) wild salmon fillet(s)
Salt and very finely ground black or white pepper
2 to 3 tablespoons all-purpose or rice flour for dredging (optional)
1 to 2 tablespoons neutral oil
¾ cup finely diced fennel, plus (optional) 1 tablespoon chopped fennel fronds
3 cloves garlic, chopped
¼ teaspoon red chile flakes, or to taste
2 tablespoons extra-dry vermouth or dry white wine
½ cup finely diced tomato
Finely grated zest of 1 small orange (about 1½ teaspoons)
¼ cup extra-virgin olive oil

PREP

Heat the oven to 425°F/220°C.

Soak the saffron threads in the warm water to help the flavor "bloom."

Rub your hand gently along the top of the fish to check for bones. If any remain, pull them out with tweezers. The fish can be cut into individual fillets if desired or left whole and served family-style, if it fits in the skillet. Pat the salmon dry and season generously with salt and pepper. Dredge it in the flour, if using, and pat off the excess.

SEAR

Heat a large ovenproof skillet over medium-high heat. When it is hot, swirl in just enough neutral oil to coat the bottom. Arrange the fish in the pan; if the fillet has been cut into pieces, make sure they are evenly spaced. The fish should each sizzle the moment it hits the hot oil. (If there is not enough room in the pan for all of the pieces, cook them in batches, wiping the pan clean and starting with fresh oil as needed.) Sear until the salmon is browned on the first side, 3 to 4 minutes.

Flip the fillets and place the skillet in the oven to cook the fish through. Fillets under 1 inch/2.5 cm should cook in 2 to 4 minutes; thicker fillets will take longer. Check for doneness: The fish should be starting to flake but still be very slightly translucent in the center. It will continue to cook slightly as it rests.

The pan handle will be very hot, so be sure to use an oven mitt from this point on. Lift the fish out of the skillet onto a clean platter or plates and keep warm while you make the sauce.

SAUCE

Discard the cooking oil and analyze the residue. Remove any unappealing bits. Return the pan to medium-high heat, add a small amount of fresh oil, and sauté the fennel until tender, about 2 minutes. Add the garlic and chile flakes and cook for about 20 seconds. Stir in the vermouth and use a wooden spoon to soften and dissolve any residue on the bottom of the pan. Add the tomatoes, orange zest, and the saffron and water mixture and simmer until the liquid has reduced and concentrated but the tomatoes retain some of their shape and texture, 1½ to 2 minutes. Stir in the extra-virgin olive oil. Taste and adjust the seasoning with salt, pepper, and/or chile flakes as needed.

Spoon the sauce over the fish, sprinkle with the chopped fennel fronds, if you have them, and serve.

Salmon with Warm Ginger-Miso Vinaigrette

Vinaigrettes can be used as simple, flavorful deglazing liquids. This is one I often have in the refrigerator. It is oil-free and good for lots of different applications. Mild white (shiro) miso is widely available, but I like the intensity of darker miso. Be sure and heap the dish with plenty of sliced scallions (or chives) as a fresh counternote to the salty sauce and fatty fish.

THIS SAUCE ALSO GOES WELL WITH: black cod, shrimp, cross-cut short ribs, and tofu (refer to the tables on pages 208–26 for cooking tips).

YIELD: 2 LARGE OR 4 MODERATE SERVINGS

1 to 1½ lbs (450 to 675 g)
   wild salmon fillet(s)
Salt and very finely ground
   black or white pepper
2 to 3 tablespoons rice flour
   or all-purpose flour for
   dredging (optional)
2 tablespoons finely minced,
   grated, or mashed fresh ginger
⅓ cup unseasoned rice vinegar
⅓ cup mirin (sweet
   Japanese rice wine)
2 tablespoons miso (see headnote)
2 tablespoons water
2 tablespoons neutral oil
¼ cup finely sliced scallion
   greens or fresh chives

PREP

Heat the oven to 425°F/220°C.

Rub your hand gently along the top of the salmon to check for bones. If any remain, pull them out with tweezers. The fish can be cut into individual fillets or left whole and served family-style, if it fits in the skillet. Pat the fish dry and season lightly with salt and pepper. (The sauce is very salty, so use less than usual.) Dredge the fish in the flour, if using, and pat off the excess.

Stir together the ginger, vinegar, mirin, miso, and water in a small bowl and set aside.

SEAR

Heat a large ovenproof skillet over medium-high heat. When it is hot, swirl in just enough oil to coat the bottom. Arrange the fish in the pan; if the fillet has been cut into pieces, make sure they are evenly spaced. The fish should sizzle the moment it hits the hot oil. (If there is not enough room in the pan for all of the pieces, sear them in batches, wiping the pan clean and starting with fresh oil as needed.) Sear until the salmon is browned on the first side, 3 to 4 minutes.

Flip the fillets and place the pan in the oven for 2 to 3 minutes; thick fillets will take a bit longer. Check for doneness: The fish should be starting to flake but still be very slightly translucent in the center. It will continue to cook as it rests.

The pan handle will be very hot, so be sure to use an oven mitt from this point on. Lift the fish out of the pan onto a clean platter or plates and keep warm while you make the sauce.

SAUCE

Discard the cooking oil, analyze the pan residue, and remove any unappealing bits. Pour the miso mixture into the pan and return it to medium-high heat. Use a wooden spoon to soften and dissolve any brown residue on the bottom of the pan. Simmer the sauce until it thickens and becomes concentrated and slightly sticky, 2 to 3 minutes.

Spoon the sauce over the salmon, sprinkle with the scallions, and serve.

CRISPY FISH SKIN

To get crispy skin when you are searing fish, the skin must be cleaned and dried very well. I often dredge the fish lightly in flour, rice flour, or cornstarch, which both protects the exposed tender flesh and helps to crisp up the skin. Be sure to heat the pan thoroughly before swirling in the oil. The thinner the pieces of fish, the hotter the pan. Place the fillets skin side down in the pan and press gently on them with a spatula for full surface contact if they start to curl or buckle. Flip them when the skin is dark brown and crisp and then cook through. I finish thicker fillets by pan-roasting them in a hot oven. Whole fish, like large trout, need to be started at a gentle sizzle, or the skin may burn before the fish is cooked through. In any case, each piece or fillet must have lots of space, so cook the fish in batches if necessary. After the skin is crisped, you want it to remain dry—serve the fish skin-side up, with sauce alongside, or spooned on at the very last minute.

Rockfish Fillets with Chinese
Sausage and Scallion Oil

Rockfish Fillets with Chinese Sausage and Scallion Oil

Chinese sausage (*lap cheong*) is a staple in our house. It has a texture similar to that of dry salami, but the taste is sweet and mild. I cut it into thin slices or matchsticks and scatter them into rice, vegetables, or main dishes. This is a recipe I make so often I almost do it unconsciously—and with a thousand small variations.

I caught a lot of spiny rockfish in the Puget Sound when I was growing up. When we hauled in a red one, we called it a snapper. I understand now that true snappers are more of a warm-water delicacy. I still tend to use the terms interchangeably, and I even see rockfish fillets sold as snapper here and there. It isn't a ruse, it's just the local vernacular.

THIS SAUCE ALSO GOES WELL WITH: salmon, chicken, eggplant, and tofu (refer to the tables on pages 208–26 for cooking tips).

YIELD: 2 LARGE OR 4 MODERATE SERVINGS

1 to 1½ pounds (450 to 675 g) rockfish or snapper fillets

Salt and very finely ground black or white pepper

2 to 3 tablespoons rice flour or cornstarch for dredging

¼ cup peanut or neutral oil

½ link Chinese sausage (*lap cheong*), rinsed and cut into slivers

2 to 3 cloves garlic, sliced

1 teaspoon minced fresh ginger

¼ teaspoon red chile flakes, or to taste

½ cup sliced scallion greens

1 teaspoon toasted sesame oil

PREP

Rub your hand gently along the top of the fillet to check for bones. If any remain, follow their path and determine how they align, then use a small sharp knife to cut them out in a thin strip. (If you and your diners don't mind fish with bones, leave them.) Pat the fish dry and season generously with salt and pepper. Dredge the fish in the rice flour and pat off any excess.

SEAR

Heat a large skillet over medium-high heat. When it is hot, swirl in just enough oil to coat the bottom. Arrange the fillets in the pan so they are evenly spaced. They should sizzle the moment they hit the hot oil. (If there is not enough room in the pan for all of the fish, sear them in batches, wiping the pan clean and starting with fresh oil as needed.) Sear the fillets until they are golden brown on the first side, about 3 minutes. Flip the fillets, reduce the heat slightly, and continue to cook for 3 to 4 minutes, until the fish is starting to flake but is still very slightly translucent

> *continues on next page*

at the thickest point; thick fillets will take longer. The fish will continue to cook through as it rests. Lift the fish out of the pan onto a clean platter or individual plates and keep warm while you make the sauce.

SAUCE

Discard the cooking oil and analyze the pan residue. Remove any unappealing bits. Add the remaining oil to the pan. Stir-fry the sausage slivers, garlic, ginger, and chile flakes until the sausage starts to curl and the garlic is aromatic but not browned, 30 seconds to 1 minute. Add the scallion greens and stir to mix. Letting the scallions warm through will help make the sauce more cohesive. Taste and adjust the seasoning with salt and pepper if needed.

Spoon the sauce over the fish fillets, drizzle with the sesame oil, and serve.

Halibut with Coarse Mustard and Rosemary Sauce

I've been serving variations of this dish for years, and it remains one of my favorites. Although halibut is a relatively mild fish, the firm texture makes it hearty enough to stand up to bold sauces. Keep in mind that halibut has a very small window between undercooked and overcooked. Do your best to cook it until the flakes are just loosening at the thickest point, then let it rest and allow the carry-over heat to finish it. It is too precious to serve dry. You can adjust the taste and texture of the sauce by adding or reducing the amount of butter. Sometimes I like this sauce coarse, robust, and thick, other times I want it silky and flowing.

THIS SAUCE ALSO GOES WELL WITH: sturgeon, cod, chicken, pork chops, steaks, vegetarian sausages, and portobello mushroom caps (refer to the tables on pages 208–26 for cooking tips).

**YIELD: 2 LARGE OR
4 MODERATE SERVINGS**

1 to 1½ pounds (450 to 675 g)
   halibut fillet(s)

2 to 3 tablespoons all-purpose or
   rice flour for dredging (optional)

Salt and finely ground black
   or white pepper

About 2 tablespoons neutral
   oil or clarified butter

⅓ cup dry white wine, such
   as Sauvignon Blanc or Pinot
   Gris, or extra-dry vermouth

1 tablespoon whole-grain mustard

2 teaspoons Dijon mustard

2 teaspoons prepared horseradish

1 teaspoon finely chopped
   fresh rosemary

2 to 3 tablespoons cold unsalted
   butter, cut into pats or small
   cubes (or substitute olive oil)

Lemon wedges for garnish

PREP

Heat the oven to 425°F/220°C.

The halibut can be cut into individual portions or left whole and served family-style, if it fits in the skillet. Pat dry and season generously with salt and pepper. Dredge the fish in the flour, if using, and pat off the excess.

SEAR

Heat a large ovenproof skillet over medium-high heat. When it is hot, swirl in just enough oil to coat the bottom. Arrange the fillets in the pan so they are evenly spaced. They should sizzle the moment they hit the hot oil. (If there is not enough room in the pan for all of the pieces, sear them in batches, wiping the pan clean and starting with fresh oil as needed.) Sear the fillets until they are golden brown on the first side, about 3 minutes.

Flip the fillets and put the pan in the oven. Fillets that are about 1 inch/2.5 cm will take 3 to 4 minutes in the oven; thicker fillets will take longer. Check for doneness: The flakes should be loose but the fish should remain very slightly translucent at the thickest point. The fillets will continue to cook slightly as they rest.

> *continues on next page*

The pan handle will be very hot, so be sure to use an oven mitt from this point on. Lift the fish out of the pan onto a clean platter or plates and keep warm while you make the sauce.

SAUCE

Discard the cooking oil and analyze the pan residue. Remove any unappealing bits. Deglaze the pan with the white wine. Use a wooden spoon to soften and dissolve any brown residue on the bottom of the pan. Increase the temperature and simmer the wine until the aroma of raw alcohol has cooked off and the volume has reduced by half. Stir in the mustards, horseradish, rosemary, and any juices that have collected under the halibut and bring just to a simmer. Gradually stir in the butter, a few pieces at a time, until just melted (or add enough olive oil to make it saucy); do not boil after the butter has been added. Taste and adjust the seasoning with salt and pepper as necessary.

Spoon just enough sauce over the fish to moisten it; serve the remainder alongside. Garnish the dish with lemon wedges and serve.

Halibut with Coarse Mustard and Rosemary Sauce (page 49), served alongside wild greens and radishes

Snapper with Tomato, Green Chile, and Citrus Sauce

In this recipe, fish fillets are "smothered" in the sauce to cook through, which means it requires a larger volume of sauce than other recipes. All that sauce is perfect for sopping up with corn tortillas and/or rice. Snapper is traditionally used in Veracruz-style recipies. I buy whatever tender white fish fillets look most appealing.

THIS SAUCE ALSO GOES WELL WITH: cod, catfish, mahi mahi, shrimp, and chicken (refer to the tables on pages 208–26 for cooking tips).

YIELD: 4 SERVINGS

1½ to 2 pounds (675 to 900 g) snapper or rockfish fillets

Salt and very finely ground black or white pepper

2 to 3 tablespoons all-purpose or rice flour for dredging

About 2 tablespoons neutral oil

½ cup chopped white onion

½ cup roasted, peeled, and chopped green chiles, such as Hatch, Anaheim, or jalapeños (or substitute one 4-ounce-/115-g can chopped jalapeño or other green chiles)

1 cup diced tomatoes (canned diced tomatoes in juice are fine)

Finely grated zest of 1 small orange (about 1½ teaspoons)

Finely grated zest of 1 lime (about 1 teaspoon)

½ cup freshly squeezed orange juice

¼ cup freshly squeezed lime juice

1 bay leaf

> *continues on next page*

PREP

Rub your hand gently along the top of the fillet to check for bones. If any remain, follow their path and determine how they align, then use a small sharp knife to cut them out in a thin strip. (If you and your diners don't mind fish with bones, leave them.) Pat the fish dry and season generously with salt and pepper. Dredge in the flour and pat off the excess.

SEAR

Heat a large skillet over medium-high heat. When it is hot, swirl in just enough oil to coat the bottom. Arrange the fillets in the pan so they are evenly spaced. They should sizzle the moment they touch the pan. (If there is not enough room in the pan for all of the fish, sear them in batches, wiping the pan clean and starting with fresh oil as needed.) Sear until the fillets are golden brown on the first side, about 3 minutes. Try to resist peeking as much as possible so the tender fillets don't break up from the agitation. Flip, reduce the heat slightly, and brown the other side; the fillets may not be cooked through at this point. Lift the fish from the pan onto a platter or plates.

1 teaspoon granulated
     sugar (optional)
½ teaspoon dried oregano
Several dashes of hot sauce,
     such as Tapatío, Cholula,
     or Tabasco, or to taste
2 tablespoons thinly sliced
     scallion greens
Cilantro sprigs and lime
     wedges for garnish

SAUCE

Discard the cooking oil and analyze the pan residue. Remove any unappealing bits or scorched flour. Return the skillet to medium heat and add a little more oil if it is dry. Add the onions and sauté until tender, about 2 minutes. Add the chiles, tomatoes, orange and lemon zests and juice, bay leaf, sugar, and oregano. Bring the sauce to a simmer and cook until it has reduced to the consistency of a chunky salsa, about 3 minutes.

Return the fish fillets and any collected juices to the skillet, gently nestling the fish in the sauce and spooning some of it over each fillet. Simmer until the fish flakes have loosened at the thickest point, 2 to 3 minutes; thicker fillets will take more time. Taste and adjust the seasoning with salt and pepper, along with a few good dashes of hot sauce.

Lift the fish onto a serving platter or plates and spoon plenty of sauce over it; serve any extra alongside. Scatter on the scallions, garnish with cilantro sprigs and lime wedges, and serve.

Cod with Warm Beet, Sour Cream, and Dill Sauce

The bright fuchsia color of this sauce is a real attention getter. The taste is equally intriguing: creamy with hints of earthiness and tang. It goes particularly well with cold-water fish. I like the sauce thick, served almost in dollops, but it is easily thinned with a splash of milk. It holds well, so it can be made early and rewarmed. Just don't boil it, or the sour cream may curdle.

THIS SAUCE ALSO GOES WELL WITH: sturgeon, walleye, chicken thighs, pork chops, and smoked sausages (refer to the tables on pages 208–26 for cooking tips).

YIELD: 2 LARGE OR 4 MODERATE SERVINGS

1 to 1½ pounds (450 to 675 g) cod fillets

Salt and very finely ground white pepper

2 to 3 tablespoons all-purpose flour for dredging

About 2 tablespoons neutral oil or clarified butter

½ cup water

¼ cup minced onion

½ cup grated cooked beets (about 1 medium or 2 small beets)

2 tablespoons apple cider vinegar or red wine vinegar

½ cup sour cream, stirred until smooth

2 tablespoons chopped fresh dill

1 tablespoon prepared horseradish

1 tablespoon whole milk (optional)

1 tablespoon vodka (optional)

PREP

Pat the cod fillets dry and season generously with salt and pepper. Dredge in the flour and pat off any excess.

SEAR

Heat a lidded sauté pan over medium-high heat. When it is hot, swirl in just enough oil to coat the bottom. Arrange the fillets in the pan so they are evenly spaced. They should sizzle the moment they hit the hot oil. (If there is not enough room in the pan for all of them, cook them in batches, wiping the pan clean and starting with fresh oil as needed.) Sear the cod until golden brown on the first side, about 3 minutes. Flip, add the water, and quickly cover the pan. Let the fish steam for 3 to 4 minutes. Check for doneness: The flakes should be loose but the thickest part of the fillets should remain just barely translucent; thick fillets will take a few minutes longer. Add additional water if needed.

Lift the fish out of the pan onto a clean platter or individual plates. Keep warm while you make the sauce.

SAUCE

Return the skillet to medium heat and cook any remaining liquid into a dry residue. Add a small amount of oil and sauté the onions until just translucent, about 2 minutes. Stir in the beets. Deglaze the pan with the vinegar, being careful to avert your face so you don't inhale the fumes and start coughing. Use a wooden spoon to gently dissolve any brown residue that remains on the bottom of the pan. Reduce the vinegar until the pan is nearly dry.

Remove the skillet from the heat and gradually stir in the sour cream, half the dill, and the horseradish. Add any juices that have collected under the cod. Season with salt and pepper and heat the sauce gently until it is just warmed through; do not let it boil. This is a thick sauce. If you prefer it thinner, add a tablespoon of milk. Add the vodka, if using, then taste and adjust the seasoning with salt, pepper, and more horseradish if you like.

Spoon the sauce onto the fish, sprinkle with the remaining dill, and serve.

Sea Bass with Fresh Fennel and Grapefruit Beurre Blanc

This lovely pale pink butter sauce, which has the tang and slight bitterness of grapefruit and the licorice hints of fennel and tarragon, pairs especially well with fish. I like it with clear, distinctive pieces of fennel and grapefruit. If you prefer a more subtle, refined sauce, finely mince the embellishments or strain the sauce before serving. "Suprême" is the term for jewel-like citrus segments that have all of the pith and membranes removed.

"Sea bass" tends to be used as an umbrella term for many varieties of sweet white-fleshed ocean fish. Ask your fishmonger for cooking tips if you aren't sure which variety you have.

THIS SAUCE ALSO GOES WELL WITH: salmon, sole, and scallops (refer to the tables on pages 208–26 for cooking tips).

YIELD: 2 LARGE OR 4 MODERATE SERVINGS

1 to 1½ pounds (450 to 675 g) sea bass fillets (skin on or off)

Salt and finely ground white pepper

2 to 3 tablespoons all-purpose or rice flour for dredging (optional)

About 2 tablespoons clarified butter or neutral oil

1 cup thinly sliced fennel

1 teaspoon finely grated grapefruit zest

1 cup freshly squeezed grapefruit juice

2 tablespoons cold unsalted butter, cut into pats or small cubes

1 teaspoon chopped fresh tarragon

8 to 12 grapefruit suprêmes (segments with all the pith and membranes removed; optional)

PREP

If the fillets are thicker than 1 inch, heat the oven to 425°F/218°C.

Rub your hand gently along the top of the fillet to check for bones. If any remain, follow their path and determine how they align, then use a small sharp knife to cut them out in a thin strip. (If you and your diners don't mind fish with bones, leave them.) Pat the fish dry and season generously with salt and white pepper. Dredge in the flour, if using, and pat off the excess.

SEAR

Heat a large ovenproof skillet over medium-high heat. When it is hot, swirl in just enough clarified butter to coat the bottom. Arrange the fish in the pan so the fillets are evenly spaced. They should sizzle the moment they hit the hot oil. (If there is not enough room in the pan for all of the pieces, sear them in batches, wiping the pan clean and starting with fresh butter as needed.) Sear the fillets until golden brown on the first side, about 3 minutes.

If the fillets are quite thin, flip them and cook through on the stovetop. Otherwise, flip the fillets and place the pan in the oven for about 3 minutes; thick fillets will take longer. Check for doneness: The fish should be starting to flake but still be very slightly translucent in the center. The fillets will continue to cook slightly as they rest.

If you finished the fish in the oven, the pan handle will be very hot, so be sure to use an oven mitt from this point on. Lift the fish out of the pan onto a clean platter or individual plates and keep warm while you make the sauce.

SAUCE

Discard the cooking fat and analyze the pan residue. Remove any unappealing bits. Return the skillet to medium heat and add any remaining clarified butter, then add the fennel and cook until just wilted. Add the grapefruit zest and juice and simmer until the fennel is very tender and the liquid is reduced to a dark syrup, about 4 minutes. Stir in the tarragon. Gradually add the butter, a few pieces at a time, until just melted. Taste and adjust the seasoning with salt as needed.

Spoon the sauce over the fish, garnish with the grapefruit suprêmes, and serve.

Mahi Mahi with Fresh Mango and Chile Chutney, served alongside fried noodles and pea pods

Mahi Mahi with Fresh Mango and Chile Chutney

I think mahi mahi is underappreciated. It is a firm, flavorful, and affordable fish. It does have a slightly gray color, which may be why it is sometimes passed over, but a bright, colorful sauce like this really livens it up. Wild fish caught in American waters are the best choice for sustainability.

THIS SAUCE ALSO GOES WELL WITH: tuna steaks, snapper, fish cakes, chicken, pork chops, tofu, and tempeh (refer to the tables on pages 208–26 for cooking tips).

YIELD: 2 LARGE OR 4 MODERATE SERVINGS

1 to 1½ pounds (450 to 675 g) mahi mahi fillets

Salt and finely ground black or white pepper

2 to 3 tablespoons all-purpose flour or rice flour for dredging (optional)

3 tablespoons peanut, coconut, or neutral oil

½ cup chopped red onion

1 to 2 red serrano chiles, seeded and chopped (or substitute Thai bird, red jalapeño, or Fresno chiles if you prefer), or to taste

2 to 3 cloves garlic, chopped

2 teaspoons minced fresh ginger

1½ cups peeled, pitted, and diced mango

2 tablespoons unseasoned rice vinegar or freshly squeezed lime juice

2 tablespoons brown sugar or grated palm sugar

> *continues on next page*

PREP

If the fillets are thicker than 1 inch/2.5 cm, heat the oven to 425°F/220°C.

Pat the fish dry and season generously with salt and pepper. Dredge in the flour, if using, and pat off the excess.

SEAR

Heat a large ovenproof skillet over medium-high heat. When it is hot, swirl in enough oil to coat the bottom. Arrange the fish in the pan so the pieces are evenly spaced. They should sizzle the moment they hit the hot oil. (If there is not enough room in the pan for all of the pieces, cook them in batches, wiping the pan clean and starting with fresh oil as needed.) Sear the fillets until golden brown on the first side, about 3 minutes.

Flip the fillets, and, if they are relatively thin, reduce the temperature slightly and cook through on the stovetop, flipping occasionally. Or put the pan in the oven and cook for 2 to 3 minutes; thick fillets will take slightly longer. Check for doneness: The fish flakes should be loose at the thickest point but still very slightly translucent. The fish will continue to cook slightly as it rests.

If you finished the fish in the oven, the pan handle will be very hot, so be sure to use an oven mitt from this point on. Transfer the fish to a clean platter or individual plates and keep warm while you make the sauce.

> *continues on next page*

1 to 2 tablespoons water,
   or as needed
1½ teaspoons cornstarch or potato
   starch, stirred together with
   1 tablespoon cold water
   until smooth
1 to 2 tablespoons sliced scallion
   greens
   or coarsely chopped fresh cilantro

SAUCE

Discard the cooking oil and analyze the pan residue. Remove any unappealing bits. Return the skillet to medium heat and add the remaining oil. Add the onions and sauté just until they start to soften. Add the chiles, garlic, and ginger and cook for about 30 seconds longer. Stir in the mangoes, add the vinegar and brown sugar, and use a wooden spoon to dissolve any brown residue on the bottom of the pan. Simmer until the mangoes are warmed through but not falling apart, about 1 minute. Add some water if needed to make the chutney saucier.

Stir the starch and water mixture thoroughly and add half of it to the pan. Bring the sauce to a boil, check on the thickness, and add some or all of the remaining starch if you prefer a thicker, stickier sauce. Once the sauce boils and becomes clear, the starch will be cooked. Stir in the scallion greens. Taste and adjust the seasoning with salt and/or chile.

Spoon the sauce over the fish and serve.

Panfried Whole Pompano
with Spiced Coconut Oil

I love whole small fish. I like to nibble the crispy skin and treasure-hunt for choice morsels. Pan-sized pompano are particularly good for cooking in a skillet. Sometimes called butterfish, they are flat, round, quick-cooking, and mild flavored. I'm perfectly happy polishing one off myself, but as a rule I serve them as a shared entrée along with several side dishes and rice. Virtually any skillet-sized whole fish can be prepared like this. Try fresh sardines, smelt, trout, mackerel, even tilapia. Cooking times will vary, of course. Fresh curry leaves can be found at Indian and some Asian markets; frozen leaves can be substituted here.

THIS SAUCE ALSO GOES WELL WITH: mahi mahi, mackerel, paneer, tofu, and chicken (refer to the tables on pages 208–26 for cooking tips).

YIELD: 1 OR 2 SERVINGS

1 to 1½ pounds (450 to 675 g)
   whole gutted and cleaned skillet-
   sized fish, such as pompano
Salt and freshly ground black pepper
About ¼ cup all-purpose or
   rice flour for dredging
⅓ cup coconut oil
1 teaspoon cumin seeds
1 teaspoon black mustard seeds
1 large shallot, thinly sliced
2 teaspoons finely minced ginger
¼ cup fresh or frozen curry leaves
1½ teaspoons hot chile powder or
   cayenne pepper, or to taste, or
   1 tablespoon minced fresh red chile
½ teaspoon ground turmeric
   (or substitute 1 to 2 teaspoons
   grated fresh turmeric)
Cilantro sprigs for garnish (optional)

PREP

If you are cooking one large fish, heat the oven to 425°F/220°C.

Use a sharp knife to cut 2 or 3 slashes in both sides of the fish to help the heat and spices penetrate the flesh. Pat the fish dry and season inside and out with salt and pepper. Dredge the fish in the flour and pat off the excess.

SEAR

Heat a large skillet (ovenproof if you are cooking one large fish) over medium heat. When it is hot, add about 3 tablespoons of the coconut oil and swirl to generously coat the bottom of the pan. Place the fish in the skillet. It should gently sizzle the moment it touches the hot oil. (If you are cooking several small fish and there is not enough room in the pan for them, cook them in batches, wiping the pan clean and starting with fresh oil if the residue seems burnt.) Sear the fish, turning often, until the skin is brown and crispy on both sides. If you are cooking one large fish, pop it into the oven to cook through. Check for doneness: The flesh in the thickest parts of the fish, along the backbone and toward the

> *continues on next page*

collar, should be starting to flake and loosen. A single small pompano will take about 10 minutes. The fish will continue to cook slightly as it rests.

If you finished the fish in the oven, the pan handle will be very hot, so be sure to use an oven mitt from this point on. Lift the fish from the pan onto a clean platter or plate. (Do not cover it, or the skin will soften.)

SAUCE

Discard the cooking oil and let the pan cool slightly, then wipe out any burnt flour. Return the skillet to medium-high heat and add the remaining coconut oil. Sprinkle in the cumin and mustard seeds and cook until they start to pop. Add the shallot and sauté until golden. Stir in the ginger and curry leaves and cook until the shallots have browned and the curry leaves are crisp, 2 to 3 minutes. Stir in the chile powder and turmeric and season with salt and pepper.

Spoon the sauce over the fish. I like this dish on the slightly salty side, so I sprinkle salt over the entire fish after it is sauced. Scatter cilantro sprigs on top, if using, and serve.

Panfried Whole Pompano
with Spiced Coconut Oil
(page 61)

Sole with Simple White Wine Sauce

This elementary white wine pan sauce is subtle and buttery, with the acidity of dry wine and the perfume of shallots and fresh herbs. Pepper on white fish is taboo to many purists; when I was in culinary school, black specks on fish fillets resulted in an instant failure. I agree that coarse black pepper is inappropriate here, but I like the light bite of the spice, so I use very finely ground white pepper.

THIS SAUCE ALSO GOES WELL WITH: Arctic char, shrimp, oysters, and veal or chicken scaloppini (refer to the tables on pages 208–26 for cooking tips).

YIELD: 2 SERVINGS

8 to 10 ounces (225 to
   285 g) sole fillets
Salt
Very finely ground white
   pepper (optional)
2 to 3 tablespoons all-purpose
   or rice flour for dredging
2 tablespoons clarified butter
   or neutral oil, or as needed
1 tablespoon minced shallot
1 clove garlic, minced (optional)
½ cup dry white wine, such as
   Sauvignon Blanc or Pinot Gris
1 to 2 tablespoons cold unsalted
   butter, cut into pats or small cubes
1 tablespoon snipped fresh chives
   or chopped fresh chervil
A splash of freshly squeezed
   lemon juice (optional)
Lemon wedges for garnish

PREP

Pat the fish fillets dry and season with salt and with pepper, if desired. Dredge the sole in the flour and pat off any excess.

SEAR

Heat a large skillet over medium-high heat. When it is hot, add enough clarified butter to coat the bottom. Arrange the fillets in the pan so they are evenly spaced. They should sizzle the moment they touch the hot butter. (If there is not enough room in the pan for all of the fish, cook it in batches, wiping the pan clean and starting with fresh butter as needed.) Cook the sole until golden brown on the first side, then carefully flip with a long spatula and cook on the other side only until the fish just starts to flake at the thickest point. Thin sole fillets may take only 2 minutes to cook through; thicker fillets may take 3 or 4. They will continue to cook slightly as they rest. Remove the skillet from the heat and lift the sole onto a serving platter or plates.

SAUCE

Discard the cooking fat and analyze the pan residue. Remove any unappealing bits and cool the pan slightly, then return the skillet to medium heat and swirl in a little fresh clarified butter. Add the shallot and cook until soft, about 1 minute. Add the garlic and cook for 20 to 30 seconds, until the aroma blooms but the garlic has not browned. Deglaze the pan with the wine. Use a wooden spoon to dissolve any residue on the bottom of the pan, then increase the heat and simmer until the aroma of raw alcohol is cooked off and the liquid is reduced to just a few tablespoons. Gradually add the cold butter, a few pieces at a time, just until melted.

At this point, you can add the chives, or you can strain the sauce so it is smooth and use the chives as a garnish. Taste the sauce and adjust the seasoning with salt, pepper, and/or a touch of lemon if you like.

Spoon the sauce over the sole and serve immediately, with lemon wedges alongside.

"Campground" Trout
with Sweet Onions and Bacon Drippings

One of my mother's favorite foods was panfried freshly caught trout or young salmon, cooked over a camp stove with onions, bacon, and the occasional Douglas fir needle that dropped from the skies. I'm an enthusiastic but mediocre catch-and-release angler, so if I were to limit my trout consumption to only campsites, I might never enjoy it again. Luckily, environmentally friendly farm-raised trout are now readily available, so I can satiate my cravings indoors rather than outside. I add maple syrup because my mother often served this dish for breakfast, and the flavor seems natural to me.

THIS SAUCE ALSO GOES WELL WITH: salmon, steelhead, chicken, pork, and broccoli (refer to the tables on pages 208–26 for cooking tips).

YIELD: 2 SERVINGS

3 to 4 strips bacon, sliced into slivers
1 to 1½ pounds (450 to 675 g) whole trout (1 large or 2 small), cleaned and head(s) removed
Salt and freshly ground black pepper
About ¼ cup all-purpose or rice flour for dredging
2 tablespoons neutral oil
1 cup thinly sliced sweet onion, such as Walla Walla Sweet
Pinch of red chile flakes (optional)
2 to 3 tablespoons beer, dry white wine, apple juice, or water
2 tablespoons pure maple syrup (optional)
2 to 3 dashes Tabasco

PREP

Heat a large lidded skillet over medium heat. Add the bacon and slowly fry it until it is very crisp. (Cooking it slowly thoroughly renders the bacon fat.) Save both the bacon and the drippings by pouring everything into a strainer set over a heatproof container.

Pat the fish dry and season it inside and out with salt and pepper. Dredge the fish in the flour and pat off the excess.

SEAR

Return the skillet to medium-high heat. When the pan is hot, swirl in the oil and arrange the fish in the skillet. The fish should sizzle gently as soon as it touches the hot oil. Cover the pan and fry the fish until it is golden brown and crisp on the first side, about 4 minutes, then carefully flip and cook on the other side. Continue cooking, flipping the fish every 2 to 3 minutes, until the skin is dark and crisp and the flesh at the thickest parts of the fish, along the backbone and toward the collar, start to loosen into flakes. Small trout will take 10 to 12 minutes; one large trout will take roughly 13 to 15 minutes total. The fish will continue to cook slightly as it rests.

Lift the fish from the pan onto a plate or platter.

SAUCE

Discard the cooking oil and analyze the pan residue. Because of the residual fond from the bacon and the flour on the fish, there is a good chance the residue will be blackened and bitter. If so, cool the pan, rinse it clean, and pat dry. Return the skillet to medium-high heat and add the reserved bacon fat. Stir in the onions and the chile flakes, if using, and sauté until the onions are aromatic and tender, 2 to 3 minutes. Deglaze the pan with the beer and use a wooden spoon to dissolve and soften any brown residue on the bottom of the pan. Add the bacon, maple syrup, if using, and Tabasco and season to taste with salt and pepper.

Pour the sauce over the trout and serve immediately, so the skin remains crisp.

Seared Shrimp with Amontillado Sherry and Orange Reduction, shown with salted almonds, anchovies, and assorted cheeses

Seared Shrimp with Amontillado Sherry and Orange Reduction

The trick to searing shrimp is to arrange them carefully in the hot pan; don't overcrowd them. Any juices released need to evaporate quickly, or the shrimp will simmer and steam rather than brown. The sherry adds a sweet nutty depth here, but the dominant flavors in this sauce are paprika and orange. These are excellent served as a tapa or party appetizer.

THIS SAUCE ALSO GOES WELL WITH: salmon, turkey scaloppini, split lobster tails, and calf's liver (refer to the tables on pages 208–26 for cooking tips).

YIELD: 3 OR 4 MODERATE SERVINGS

1 pound (450 g) large shrimp (size 21–25), peeled and deveined
Salt and freshly ground black pepper
About 2 tablespoons olive or neutral oil
4 cloves garlic, finely chopped
1/4 teaspoon red chile flakes, or to taste
1 teaspoon hot or mild smoked paprika (*pimentón*)
3/4 cup amontillado or other nutty medium sherry
2 teaspoons grated orange zest
1/2 cup freshly squeezed orange juice
2 tablespoons freshly squeezed lemon juice
1 tablespoon extra-virgin olive oil or cold unsalted butter
1 tablespoon chopped fresh parsley

PREP

Pat the shrimp dry and season with salt and pepper.

SEAR

Heat a large skillet over medium-high heat. When the pan is hot, add just enough oil to coat the bottom. Arrange the shrimp in the pan so they are evenly spaced. (Do not overcrowd the pan; cook the shrimp in batches if necessary, adding more oil as needed.) The shrimp should sizzle the moment they touch the hot oil. It will take only a minute for the shrimp to start to curl and turn pink and then slightly brown on the first side. Flip them and cook until they are evenly browned on the second side and curled but not quite cooked through; the whole process should take no longer than about 3 minutes. The shrimp will continue to cook slightly as they rest. Transfer them to a clean platter.

> continues on next page

SAUCE

Discard the cooking oil and analyze the pan residue. Wipe out the pan if necessary. Let the skillet cool slightly, then return it to medium heat. Add more oil if the pan is dry and sauté the garlic and chile flakes until the aroma blooms but the garlic has not browned, about 20 seconds. Stir in the paprika and immediately deglaze the pan with the sherry. Use a wooden spoon to dissolve any brown residue in the bottom of the pan. Increase the heat to high and boil to reduce the volume of the sherry by half. Add the orange zest, juice, and any juices that have collected on the platter with the shrimp and boil, stirring often, for about 5 minutes, until the liquid has concentrated into a thick, sticky glaze that clings lightly to the spoon. Add the lemon juice and olive oil. Taste and adjust the seasoning with salt and pepper.

Return the shrimp to the pan and toss to coat and warm through. Stir in the parsley, transfer to a serving dish, and serve.

Seared Scallops with Sherry Beurre Blanc, Chanterelles, and Sweet Corn

Perfectly seared scallops are well browned on the outside and barely cooked on the inside, so they remain sweet and succulent. I once heard overcooked scallops described as having the texture of pencil erasers and they are *far* too precious to end up with the culinary appeal of an office supply. This sauce is a variation on French beurre blanc—butter that is suspended in perfect liquidity and flavored with wine, or, in this case, aged sherry. If that isn't decadent enough for your liking, you can sprinkle the plates with crumbles of crisp bacon. Nothing about this recipe is particularly difficult, but it takes a bit more finesse than many of the others in the book because there are several elements to get just right.

THIS SAUCE ALSO GOES WELL WITH: salmon, sea bass, halibut, chicken breasts, and turkey or veal scaloppini, and polenta cakes (refer to the tables on pages 208–26 for cooking tips).

YIELD: 3 OR 4 SERVINGS

1 to 1½ pounds (450 to 675 g) large sea scallops (12 to 16), preferably "dry-packed"

2 tablespoons clarified butter or neutral oil

1 cup quartered or roughly chopped chanterelle mushrooms (about 2 ounces/60 g)

1 medium ear corn, husked, silks removed, and kernels cut from the cob

Salt and finely ground black pepper

3 tablespoons minced shallots

3 tablespoons sherry vinegar

⅓ cup amontillado or other nutty medium sherry

½ teaspoon chopped fresh thyme

8 tablespoons (4 ounces/115 g/1 stick) cold unsalted butter, cut into pats or small cubes

PREP

Remove and discard the adductor muscles from the scallops. (These look like small, flat bands clinging to the side of the scallops; they are very tough and do not soften during cooking.) Scallops are often soaked in brine during processing to keep them moist and plump, so I don't season them before cooking. Make sure you take the extra time to pat them dry with paper towels.

SEAR

Heat a large skillet over medium-high heat. Let the skillet get properly hot—the scallops need to brown quickly, or they can seep liquid and start to simmer or steam. Swirl in just enough clarified butter to coat the bottom of the pan. Arrange the scallops flat side down in the skillet. (Do not crowd the pan; cook the scallops in batches if necessary, adding more butter as needed.) The scallops should sizzle as soon as they touch the pan. Sear the scallops to a dark brown on the first side, about 2 minutes. If the scallops stick, they need a bit longer to cook; they will release themselves as they

> *continues on next page*

firm up. Flip, reduce the heat slightly, and cook until the scallops just start to spring back when you press them lightly in the center, 1 to 2 minutes more. They will continue to cook slightly as they rest. Transfer the scallops to a clean platter and keep warm while you finish the sauce.

SAUCE

Discard the cooking oil and analyze the pan residue. Remove any unappealing bits. Add the remaining clarified butter to the pan and sear the chanterelles over medium-high to high heat. As with the scallops, chanterelles should be browned on the outside and cooked until just tender on the inside, about 2 minutes total. If the chanterelles are very fresh and wet, you may need to cook them in smaller batches to ensure they brown well. Stir in the corn and season the mixture with a bit of salt and pepper. Sauté until the corn is tender and any raw starchy taste is gone; for very fresh sweet corn, this will take only a minute. Spoon the corn and mushroom mixture onto a warm platter or individual plates.

Cool the pan slightly, then return it to medium-high heat, add the shallots and vinegar, and simmer until the vinegar has almost completely evaporated. Add the sherry and thyme and boil to reduce the volume by half. Gradually whisk in the butter, a few pieces at a time, just until melted. Don't let the sauce boil after you add the butter. Taste and adjust the seasoning with salt and with a touch of finely ground black pepper if needed.

Spoon the sauce over the warm mushrooms and corn and top with the seared scallops. Serve immediately.

Seared Scallops with Sherry Beurre Blanc, Chanterelles, and Sweet Corn (page 71)

Calamari Steaks with Garlic, Toasted Almond, and Thyme Sauce

Thick, oval calamari "steaks" are available at many fishmongers and are remarkably inexpensive. They are cut from the mantle of large squid and usually machine-tenderized. They are meaty, with a taste of the sea mingled with a slight sweetness. I don't like squid that is rubbery, but I do like it firm, so I tend to cook it longer than some. If you like it very tender, cook the steaks for just about 1½ minutes per side.

I have included an egg coating here as well as a dip in plain flour. The egg adds color, texture, and flavor; feel free to omit it if you like. The coating doesn't adhere strongly, so be careful with the steaks when flipping them, or it can scrape off.

THIS SAUCE ALSO GOES WELL WITH: sole, swordfish, snapper, and chicken breasts (refer to the tables on pages 208–26 for cooking tips).

YIELD: 2 TO 4 SERVINGS

2 to 4 tenderized calamari steaks
   (4 to 5 ounces/115 to 140 g each)
Salt and finely ground black pepper
2 to 3 tablespoons all-purpose
   flour for dredging
2 large eggs (optional)
1 to 2 tablespoons clarified
   butter or neutral oil
3 cloves garlic, thinly sliced
¼ teaspoon red chile
   flakes, or to taste
⅓ cup dry white wine, such as
   Sauvignon Blanc or Pinot Gris
4 thin slices lemon
4 tablespoons (2 ounces/60 g/
   ½ stick) cold unsalted butter,
   cut into pats or small cubes
¼ cup toasted sliced almonds
1 teaspoon chopped fresh thyme
Lemon wedges for garnish

PREP

Pat the calamari steaks dry and season generously with salt and pepper. Dredge in the flour and pat off the excess. Crack the eggs, if using, into a shallow plate or dish and stir with a fork; adding a tiny pinch of salt will help them liquefy.

SEAR

Heat a large skillet over medium heat. When the pan is hot, add just enough clarified butter to coat the bottom. Dip one of the flour-dredged steaks in the beaten egg, if using, and immediately put it in the pan, then continue with the remaining steaks. (If there is not enough room in the skillet, dip and cook the squid steaks in batches.) The steaks should just sizzle when they touch the hot oil. Cook the calamari until well browned on the first side, 2 to 3 minutes, then use a thin flexible spatula to flip the steaks, making sure you keep the coating and calamari together. Continue to cook until the steaks have firmed up but are not rubbery, about 3 minutes more. (If you prefer your squid very tender, cook it for half that time.) Transfer the calamari to a clean platter or plates and keep warm while you make the sauce.

SAUCE

Discard the cooking oil and analyze the pan residue. Remove any unappealing bits and scorched flour. Let the pan cool slightly, then return it to medium heat. Add some butter if the pan seems dry, stir in the garlic and chile flakes, and cook for about 20 seconds, until the aroma of the garlic blooms but it has not browned. Deglaze the pan with the white wine, using a wooden spoon to dissolve any brown residue on the bottom of the skillet. Add the lemon slices and simmer until the raw alcohol aroma is gone and the wine is nearly evaporated. Gradually stir in the remaining butter, a few pieces at a time, until just melted. Stir in the almonds and thyme. Taste and adjust the seasoning with salt and pepper.

Spoon the sauce over the calamari steaks and serve immediately, with lemon wedges alongside.

Panfried Oysters with
Canadian Caesar Cocktail Reduction

Caesars are Canada's national cocktail. They are Bloody Marys made with clam nectar, or Clamato juice. When you use these elements as a deglazing liquid, you end up with perhaps the quintessential tomato "cocktail sauce" for pan-seared shellfish. It's spicy, zesty and bright, as you would expect, but flowing and smooth from the finish of butter. *Micheladas* are popular Mexican beer drinks that are also made with clam/tomato juice, and some versions of Clamato juice are spiced with lime and chiles. Classic is preferable here.

I've tried finishing this sauce with a splash of vodka, to better mimic the traditional cocktail, but it never adds more than a raw bite. I don't recommend it.

THIS SAUCE ALSO GOES WELL WITH: shrimp, calamari steaks, chicken, thin steaks, and meatballs or patties (refer to the tables on pages 208–26 for cooking tips).

YIELD: 2 OR 3 SERVINGS

12 to 18 extra-small oysters,
  shucked (jarred are fine)
¾ cup all-purpose flour
  for dredging
2 tablespoons celery salt
3 to 4 tablespoons neutral
  oil or clarified butter
1 cup plain Clamato juice (or
  ½ cup tomato juice mixed
  with ½ cup clam nectar)
2 teaspoons prepared or finely
  grated fresh horseradish
2 teaspoons Tabasco
  sauce, or to taste
1 teaspoon Worcestershire sauce
1 tablespoon freshly
  squeezed lemon juice
Freshly ground black pepper
    > *continues on next page*

PREP

Pour the oysters into a fine-mesh colander or sieve set over a bowl and leave to drain while you prepare the other ingredients.

When ready to cook the oysters, mix the flour and celery salt in a shallow dish or plate. Dredge the oysters in the seasoned flour and pat off the excess.

SEAR

Heat a large skillet over medium heat. When it is hot, swirl in just enough oil to coat the bottom. Arrange the oysters in the pan so they are evenly spaced. They should lightly sizzle the moment they hit the hot oil. Cook the oysters until they are crisp and brown on the first side, about 2 minutes. Flip and continue to cook until they are cooked to your preference. Some people like them just barely warmed through and silky in the middle, which takes no more than a minute more; I prefer them crisp on the outside and al dente inside, but never leathery, so I cook them for 2 to 3 minutes longer at this point. Lift the oysters onto a clean platter or plates, dabbing them with a paper towel if they seem at all greasy.

2 tablespoons cold unsalted butter,
cut into pats or small cubes

2 tablespoons minced celery or
stuffed green olives (optional)

Lemon wedges for garnish

SAUCE

Discard the cooking oil and analyze the pan residue. If any of the flour scorched, wipe the pan clean. Return the skillet to medium heat. Pour in the Clamato juice and use a wooden spoon to dissolve any brown residue on the bottom of the pan. Boil until the juice has reduced and thickened to the consistency of tomato soup or thin ketchup. Remove the pan from the heat and stir in the horseradish, Tabasco, Worcestershire, and lemon juice. The sauce will be quite salty, so add salt if necessary only after you have tasted it. Gradually stir in the butter, a few pieces at a time, until it is melted and creamy.

Drizzle enough sauce over the oysters to moisten them and serve the rest alongside. Scatter them with the minced celery, if using, and serve immediately, with lemon wedges.

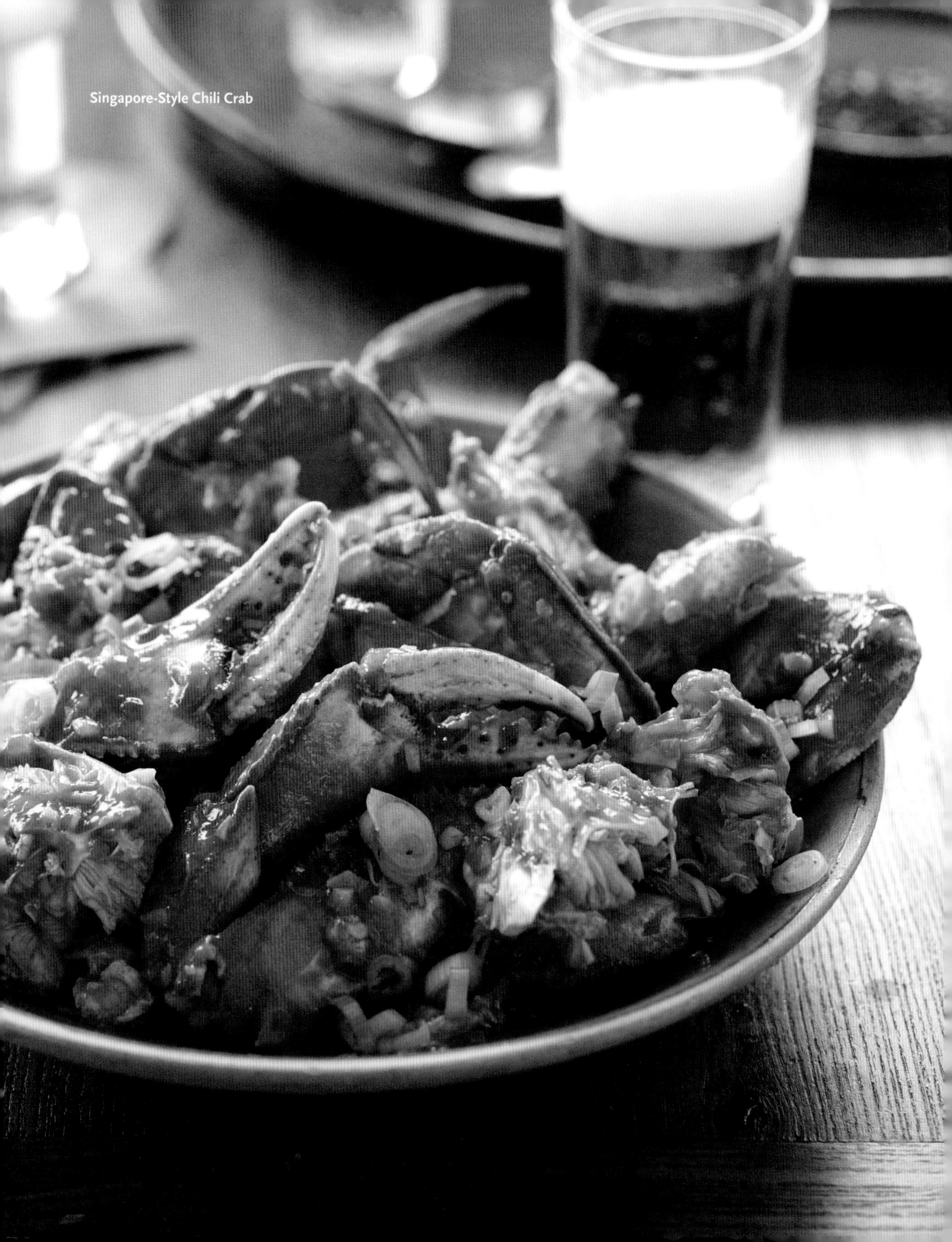

Singapore-Style Chili Crab

Singapore-Style Chili Crab

True chili crab is an event, not just a meal, and it is ALL about the sauce. I was lucky enough to slurp up the messy, authentic version in an open-air restaurant in Singapore. It was thick with spices and pungent with seasonings. This is a mock-up of the real deal. The egg may sound odd at first, but trust me, it's delicious. While this recipe doesn't follow the usual sear-and-sauce technique, I thought it would be beneficial to include a few recipes to show how truly diverse a quick pan sauce can be. Cooked whole Dungeness crab is ubiquitous where I live. If you have access to live crab, dispatch it, remove the carapace and organs, and cut or break it up into portions, then simmer the pieces in the sauce until the meat slips out of the shells, as described below.

This dish needs to be served with a thick stack of napkins and plenty of cold beer. Finger bowls are handy too.

THIS SAUCE ALSO GOES WELL WITH: shrimp, split small lobster tails, and tofu (refer to the tables on pages 208–26 for cooking tips).

YIELD: 2 SERVINGS

1 Dungeness crab, cooked, cleaned, and cracked (for live crab, see headnote)

¼ cup peanut or neutral oil

2 tablespoons minced fresh ginger

2 tablespoons minced shallots

1 tablespoon minced garlic

3 tablespoons sambal oelek, or to taste

¼ cup ketchup

2 tablespoons sugar

½ cup low-sodium chicken stock, preferably homemade

2 tablespoons fish sauce (optional)

1 teaspoon cornstarch, stirred together with 1 tablespoon cold water until smooth

Salt and freshly ground black pepper

1 egg, beaten (optional)

½ cup sliced scallion greens

Split the crab into leg and body segments.

Heat a large lidded sauté pan over medium heat. Add the oil and swirl to coat. Sauté the ginger and shallots, stirring, until softened but not browned, about 1 minute. Add the garlic and cook for about 30 seconds. Stir in the sambal oelek and let it sizzle and cook for another 30 seconds. Stir in the ketchup and sugar to mix, then add the stock and bring to a boil.

Add the crab and stir to coat the pieces evenly. Cover and simmer for 4 to 5 minutes, lifting the lid and flipping the pieces now and then to heat them through and help the sauce penetrate the cracks in the shells. (If you are using uncooked crab pieces, give them a stir every few minutes and cook until the meat slips from the shells, about 8 to 10 minutes longer.)

Remove the lid and stir in the fish sauce, if using, and the well-stirred cornstarch mixture. Taste and adjust the seasoning with salt, pepper, sugar, and/or sambal oelek.

Drizzle the beaten egg, if using, over the crab; do not stir. Cover the pan and let simmer until the egg has just cooked through, about 1 minute.

Toss the crab in the sauce again and transfer to a serving dish. Sprinkle with the sliced scallion greens and serve.

Split Lobster Tails
with Habanero Lime Butter

Enough with the drawn butter and lemon already! I like my lobsters with more vim. This is a powerful, complicated sauce inspired by the flavors of the Caribbean. Use just enough habanero chiles to give it bite. The point is not to make this crazy hot, but to add flavor. Serve a whole tail each as an entrée or serve half alongside a grilled steak for a rejuvenated "surf-and-turf" plate.

THIS SAUCE ALSO GOES WELL WITH: shrimp, grouper, tuna steaks, chicken, pork, and sweet potato planks (refer to the tables on pages 208–26 for cooking tips).

**YIELD: 2 OR 4 SERVINGS
(SEE HEADNOTE)**

2 lobster tails (4 to 6 ounces
/115 to 170 g each)
1 tablespoon coconut or neutral oil
½ cup strong ginger ale or
ginger beer, such as Reed's
2 cloves garlic, minced
½ teaspoon finely minced habanero
chile (substitute serrano or
jalapeño if you prefer), or to taste
1½ teaspoons finely grated lime zest
Pinch of ground allspice
2 tablespoons unsalted butter,
cut into pats or small cubes
2 to 3 tablespoons freshly
squeezed lime juice
Salt and freshly ground
black or white pepper
2 to 3 tablespoons toasted
coconut (optional)

PREP

To split the lobster tails, carefully place the tip of a large sharp knife at the highest point of each shell. Being very careful to keep your fingers clear of the sharp blade, pierce it straight through and then lever the knife to cut through the meat and bottom shell. Turn the tail around and repeat in the other direction to make 2 even pieces. Remove and discard the vein and any unappealing bits. Use scissors to trim off the spindly swimmerettes. If you want the lobster tails to remain straight, thread a wooden skewer lengthwise through the meat; if the skewers are long, trim them so they don't stick out more than about an inch, or you will have trouble fitting everything in the pan. Pat the lobster dry with paper towels.

SEAR

Heat a large lidded sauté pan over medium-high heat. When it is hot, swirl in enough oil to coat the bottom. Arrange the lobster tails cut side down in the pan. They should sizzle the moment they touch the hot oil. (If they don't all fit, sear them in batches, wiping the pan clean and using fresh oil as needed.) Sear the lobster until the meat is golden brown, about 2 minutes (the tails will curl as they cook if you haven't used skewers). Add the ginger ale, being careful to protect your hands and face from the steam, cover, and steam the lobster until just cooked through, 1 to 2 minutes more. The shells should be red and the meat just opaque.

Lift the lobster from the skillet onto plates or a platter, cut side up. Remove the skewers if you used them.

SAUCE

Boil the pan juices until they are reduced by half. Stir in the garlic, habanero, lime zest, and allspice and continue to reduce the sauce until concentrated and almost syrupy. Gradually add the butter, a few pieces at a time, stirring until the butter is just melted, then add the lime juice. Taste and adjust the seasoning with salt and pepper as needed.

Spoon the sauce over the lobster tails, sprinkle with the toasted coconut, if using, and serve.

CHICKEN AND POULTRY

Chicken Piccata

Chicken Piccata
(Chicken Breast Cutlets with Lemon and Caper Sauce)

This is a recipe that every cook should know. It is simple, quick, and almost universally popular. I leave the chicken in the pan while I make the pan sauce because I like the silky texture the flour-dredged cutlets develop when simmered in the lemony sauce. Some cooks prefer to cook the chicken through and transfer it to a platter before making the sauce and pouring it over the chicken so the crust remains slightly crisp.

THIS SAUCE ALSO GOES WELL WITH: pork, turkey, or veal scaloppini; swordfish; and calamari steaks (refer to the tables on pages 208–26 for cooking tips).

YIELD: 2 LARGE OR 4 MODERATE SERVINGS

1 to 1½ pounds (450 to 675 g) boneless, skinless chicken breasts (2), sliced and pounded into cutlets (see page 87)

Salt and freshly ground black pepper

2 to 3 tablespoons all-purpose or rice flour for dredging

2 tablespoons neutral oil or clarified butter

½ cup low-sodium chicken stock, preferably homemade

4 thin slices lemon

2 tablespoons freshly squeezed lemon juice

Pinch of red chile flakes (optional)

3 tablespoons cold unsalted butter, cut into pats or small cubes

2 tablespoons coarsely chopped fresh parsley

2 tablespoons drained capers, chopped if very large

PREP

Pat the chicken dry and season generously with salt and pepper. Dredge in the flour and pat off the excess.

SEAR

Heat a large skillet over medium-high heat. When the pan is hot, swirl in enough oil to coat the bottom. Arrange the chicken pieces in the pan so they are evenly spaced. They should sizzle the moment they touch the hot oil. (If there is not enough room in the pan for all the pieces, cook them in batches, wiping the pan clean and starting with fresh oil as needed.) Brown the chicken on the first side, about 3 minutes, then flip, reduce the heat slightly, and brown on the other side; the chicken will not be cooked through at this point. If you have cooked the chicken in batches, return all of the pieces to the pan.

> *continues on next page*

SAUCE

Pour in the chicken stock and gently rub the pan residue with the chicken pieces to dissolve it into the sauce. Add the lemon slices, lemon juice, and chile flakes, if using, and simmer, flipping the pieces regularly, until they are just cooked through, about 4 minutes. Lift the chicken from the pan onto a clean platter or individual serving plates.

Simmer to reduce the sauce until it is the consistency of gravy. Gradually stir in the cold butter, a few pieces at a time, until just melted. Finish the sauce with the chopped parsley and capers. Taste and adjust the salt and pepper as needed. The sauce is meant to be tart.

Spoon the sauce over the chicken and serve immediately.

TRIMMING AND POUNDING
CHICKEN BREAST CUTLETS AND SCALOPPINI

Chicken breasts cook more quickly and evenly when they are trimmed and lightly pounded to a uniform thickness. There is less risk of the chicken drying out, because all of it will be done at the same time. In my local supermarkets, organic boneless, skinless chicken breasts average between 8 and 12 ounces (225 and 340 g). You can easily make 2 or 3 cutlets from a single chicken breast. If the pieces are cut smaller or pounded thinner, they are called scaloppini.

FOR 2 CUTLETS OR SCALOPPINI: Place a boneless, skinless chicken breast on a work surface. Press down on the breast with your palm so you can feel the density of the meat and hold it stable as you slice through it. Then lift your fingers high to keep them out of the way and use a large sharp knife to slice the chicken breast horizontally in half with long, slow, even slicing motions. Separate the chicken pieces. Place them on a smooth work surface, cover with parchment paper or plastic wrap, and use a smooth meat pounder to pound them evenly into cutlets or thin scaloppini.

FOR 3 CUTLETS: This is best for very thick, tapered boneless, skinless chicken breasts. Cut the whole breast crosswise in half, on a slight diagonal, toward the smaller, tapered tip. This yields a single cutlet. The other piece will be much thicker. Slice it horizontally in half into 2 cutlets as described above. Pound all 3 pieces to an even thickness.

Chicken breasts ready to be pounded into cutlets and scaloppini

Chicken with Buttery Fresh Tomato and Basil Sauce

This is one of those dishes that I find myself making over and over again. It is very simple but incredibly satisfying. I like finishing it with butter, but a drizzle of extra-virgin olive oil takes it in another and equally appealing direction. For a softer, more refined texture, remove the skins and seeds from the tomatoes before dicing them.

THIS SAUCE ALSO GOES WELL WITH: salmon, halibut, pork scaloppini, steaks, and rustic bread slices (refer to the tables on pages 208–26 for cooking tips).

YIELD: 2 LARGE OR 4 MODERATE SERVINGS

1 to 1½ pounds (450 to 675 g) boneless, skinless chicken thighs (4 to 6), trimmed, flattened, and pounded to an even thickness of ½ inch/1.25 cm, or boneless, skinless chicken breast cutlets

Salt and finely ground black or white pepper

3 tablespoons extra-virgin or light olive oil

2 to 3 cloves garlic, chopped

¼ teaspoon red chile flakes, or to taste

1 cup diced ripe tomatoes (preferably skinned and seeded)

3 tablespoons dry white wine, such as Sauvignon Blanc or Pinot Gris, or extra-dry vermouth

2 tablespoons cold unsalted butter cut into cut into pats or small cubes

1 to 2 tablespoons coarsely chopped or torn fresh basil leaves

PREP

Pat the chicken dry and season lightly with salt and pepper.

SEAR

Heat a large skillet over medium-high heat. When it is hot, swirl in just enough oil to coat the bottom. Arrange the chicken in the pan so the pieces are evenly spaced. They should sizzle the moment they touch the hot oil. (If there is not enough room in the pan for all the pieces, cook them in batches, wiping the pan clean and starting with fresh oil if the residue seems burnt.) Sear the chicken until browned on the first side, about 3 minutes. Flip, reduce the temperature slightly, and brown the other side. Then continue to cook, flipping often, until the chicken is just cooked through, 6 to 8 minutes for boneless thighs, 3 to 4 minutes for chicken breast cutlets. Transfer the chicken to a clean platter and keep warm while you make the sauce.

SAUCE

Discard the cooking oil and cool the pan slightly. Analyze the residue and remove any unappealing bits. Return the skillet to medium heat. Add the remaining olive oil, the garlic, and chile flakes and sauté for about 20 seconds, until the aroma of the garlic has bloomed but it has not browned. Stir in the tomatoes and use a wooden spoon to dissolve any brown residue on the bottom of the pan. Add the wine and simmer until the aroma of raw alcohol has cooked off, about 1 minute. Season the sauce lightly with salt and pepper and simmer until the tomatoes have softened and become saucy but have not entirely lost their definition, about 3 minutes.

Return the chicken and any juices that have collected to the skillet. Flip the pieces to coat with the sauce as they heat through. Stir in the butter, a few pieces at a time, until just melted. Stir in the basil. Taste and adjust the seasoning with salt and pepper as needed.

Lift the chicken onto a clean platter or individual plates, spoon on the sauce, and serve.

Chicken with Garlic, Greens, and
Salty Cheese, served alongside
spaghetti squash

Chicken with Garlic, Greens, and Salty Cheese

Bonne femme is a classic French cooking term that once described recipes made with ingredients that a "good woman" would always have on hand. I ran into the term again recently and it had me wondering what today's busy cooks might create from contemporary kitchen staples. I started with a list of ingredients my friends often buy: chicken, olive oil, garlic, greens, cheese, and nuts. Then I played around until I landed on this quick, satisfying seared and sauced dish. The salty cheese can be virtually any dry, aged, or crumbly cheese. I like toasted almonds here, but pistachios, walnuts, pepitas, and pine nuts also work well.

THIS SAUCE ALSO GOES WELL WITH: salmon, whole trout, pork chops, eggplant, and rustic bread (refer to the tables on pages 208–26 for cooking tips).

**YIELD: 2 LARGE OR
4 MODERATE SERVINGS**

1 to 1½ pounds (450 to 675 g)
  boneless, skinless chicken breasts
  (2), sliced and pounded into
  thin scaloppini (see page 87)
Salt and freshly ground black pepper
2 to 3 tablespoons all-purpose or
  rice flour for dredging (optional)
About 2 tablespoons neutral,
  olive, or avocado oil
3 to 4 cloves garlic, sliced
¼ teaspoon red chile
  flakes, or to taste
2 tablespoons red wine vinegar
  or sherry vinegar
½ cup dry white wine, such as
  Sauvignon Blanc or Pinot Gris
¾ cup low-sodium chicken stock,
  preferably homemade
1 cup loosely packed chopped
  hearty greens, such as
  kale, chard, or arugula

> *continues on next page*

PREP

Pat the chicken dry and season generously with salt and pepper. Dredge in the flour, if using, and pat off the excess.

SEAR

Heat a large skillet over medium-high heat. When it is hot, swirl in enough oil to coat the bottom. Arrange the chicken in the pan so the pieces are evenly spaced. They should sizzle the moment they touch the hot oil. (If there is not enough room in the pan for all of the pieces, cook them in batches, wiping the pan clean and starting with fresh oil as needed.) Brown the chicken on the first side, about 3 minutes, then flip, reduce the heat slightly, and brown the other side. The chicken doesn't need to be completely cooked through at this point. Transfer the chicken to a clean platter and keep warm while you make the sauce.

> *continues on next page*

2 tablespoons cold unsalted
butter, cut into pats or small cubes
(or substitute extra-virgin olive oil)
2 tablespoons grated or
crumbled salty cheese, such
as feta, ricotta salata, aged
goat cheese, or Parmesan
2 tablespoons toasted almonds,
coarsely chopped (optional)

SAUCE

Discard the cooking oil and analyze the pan residue. Remove any unappealing bits or scorched flour and cool the pan slightly, then return the skillet to medium heat. Add some oil if the pan is very dry. Add the garlic and chile flakes and cook for about 20 seconds, until the aroma of the garlic has bloomed but it has not browned. Deglaze the pan with the vinegar, being careful not to inhale the fumes, or they may make you cough. Use a wooden spoon to dissolve the brown residue on the bottom of the pan. Add the wine and simmer until the aroma of raw alcohol is gone and the volume has reduced by about half. Add the chicken stock, return the chicken and any collected juices to the skillet, and simmer, flipping the chicken regularly, until it is cooked through, 3 to 4 minutes. Lift the chicken onto a clean platter or plates.

Simmer the sauce for a minute or two longer, until it is the consistency of gravy. It will thin slightly once the greens and butter are added. Stir in the greens, along with a pinch each of salt and pepper, and cook until they have just wilted but are still bright, about 30 seconds. Finish the sauce by stirring in the cold butter, a few pieces at a time, until just melted (or stir in the olive oil). Taste and adjust the seasoning with salt and pepper as needed.

Spoon the sauce onto the chicken and sprinkle with the cheese and the almonds, if using. Serve immediately.

Chicken with Hoisin Glaze and Cashews

This super-quick recipe is an example of how little time and effort it can take to turn plain chicken into something remarkable. Boneless chicken thigh meat is good here because it is softer and has more flavor than breasts. I consider hoisin sauce to be a kitchen staple. Lee Kum Kee is my preferred brand.

THIS SAUCE ALSO GOES WELL WITH: pork, turkey meatballs, semi-boneless quail, tofu, broccoli, and eggplant (refer to the tables on pages 208–26 for cooking tips).

YIELD: 2 LARGE OR 4 MODERATE SERVINGS

1 to 1½ pounds (450 to 675 g) boneless, skinless chicken thighs (4 to 6), trimmed, flattened, and pounded to an even thickness of ½ inch/ 1.25 cm, or boneless, skinless chicken breasts (2), sliced and pounded into cutlets (see page 87)

Salt and finely ground black or white pepper

1 to 2 tablespoons peanut or neutral oil

½ cup low-sodium chicken stock, preferably homemade

¼ cup hoisin sauce

½ cup lightly salted roasted cashew halves and pieces

3 tablespoons sliced scallion greens

PREP

Pat the chicken dry and season generously with salt and pepper.

SEAR

Heat a large skillet over medium-high heat. When it is hot, swirl in enough oil to coat the bottom. Arrange the chicken in the pan so the pieces are evenly spaced. They should sizzle the moment they touch the hot oil. (If there is not enough room in the pan for all of the pieces, cook them in batches, wiping the pan clean and starting with fresh oil as needed.) Brown the chicken on the first side, about 3 minutes, then flip, reduce the heat slightly, and brown the other side. The chicken will not be cooked through at this point.

SAUCE

Pour in the chicken stock and stir to dissolve any brown residue. Stir in the hoisin sauce and flip the chicken pieces to coat. Simmer, flipping occasionally, until the chicken is fully cooked and the sauce is thick and syrupy, 6 to 8 minutes for thighs, about 4 minutes for chicken breast cutlets. Add the cashews to the pan and toss to mix. Taste and adjust the seasoning as needed.

Lift the chicken onto a clean platter or individual plates. Spoon the sauce over the top, garnish with the scallions, and serve.

Chicken with Mixed Mushrooms and Marsala

Chicken or veal Marsala is an Italian-American restaurant staple. There are as many variations of the sauce as there are chefs. One friend adds minced pancetta with the onions, another adds fresh tomatoes and a touch of demi-glace. A finish of cream is popular. This is my version. I love wild mushrooms and there is no shortage of them in the Pacific Northwest. Button, cremini, and shiitake mushrooms are perfectly good if wild varieties are difficult to find or out of season. I prefer dry Marsala over sweet, but both work fine.

THIS SAUCE ALSO GOES WELL WITH: veal, pork, or turkey scaloppini; polenta cakes; and thin steaks (refer to the tables on pages 208–26 for cooking tips).

**YIELD: 2 LARGE OR
4 MODERATE SERVINGS**

1 to 1½ pounds (450 to 675 g)
    boneless, skinless chicken breasts
    (2), sliced and pounded into cutlets
    or thin scaloppini (see page 87)
Salt and freshly ground black pepper
2 to 3 tablespoons all-purpose
    flour for dredging (optional)
3 tablespoons clarified
    butter or neutral oil
2 cups sliced cleaned assorted
    mushrooms, such as cremini,
    chanterelles, shiitake, maitake,
    porcini, and/or morels(about
    5 to 6 ounces/140 to 170 g,
    depending on the varieties)
2 tablespoons minced shallots
1 cup dry Marsala (substitute
    sweet Marsala if you prefer)
¾ cup low-sodium chicken stock,
    preferably homemade
        > *continues on next page*

PREP

Pat the chicken dry and season generously with salt and pepper. Dredge the chicken in the flour, if using, and pat off the excess.

SEAR

Heat a large skillet over medium-high heat. When it is hot, swirl in enough clarified butter to coat the bottom. Arrange the chicken pieces in the pan so they are evenly spaced. They should sizzle the moment they touch the hot butter. (If there is not enough room in the pan for all of the pieces, cook the chicken in batches, wiping the pan clean and starting with fresh butter as needed.) Brown the chicken well on the first side, about 3 minutes, then flip, reduce the heat slightly, and brown on the other side. The chicken will not be cooked through at this point. Transfer the chicken to a clean platter and keep warm while you make the sauce.

2 or 3 sprigs fresh thyme or
    ½ teaspoon dried thyme
2 tablespoons cold unsalted
    butter, cut into pats or small cubes
2 tablespoons heavy cream (optional)
1 tablespoon chopped fresh parsley

SAUCE

Discard the cooking fat and analyze the pan residue. Remove any unappealing bits or scorched flour. Cool the pan slightly, then return it to medium-high heat and add the remaining clarified butter. Sauté the mushrooms until browned, about 3 minutes. Add the shallots and cook for another minute. Deglaze the pan with the Marsala, using a wooden spoon to help dissolve any flavorful residue on the bottom of the pan. Increase the heat to high and boil to reduce the volume of the wine by half.

Add the chicken stock and thyme, return the chicken and any juices that have collected to the pan, and simmer, flipping the chicken occasionally, until it is cooked through and the sauce has thickened slightly, about 5 minutes. Lift the chicken pieces onto a clean platter or individual plates.

Remove and discard the thyme sprigs, if you used them. Increase the temperature and reduce the sauce until it is the consistency of thin gravy. Gradually stir in the cold butter, a few pieces at a time, until just melted. Add the cream, if using it. Taste and adjust the seasoning with salt and pepper as needed.

Spoon the sauce over the chicken, sprinkle with the parsley, and serve.

Chicken with French Vinegar Sauce

I adore this recipe. It is inspired by *poulet au vinaigre,* a French braised chicken preparation that is tangy with vinegar and tomatoes and made rich with a touch of cream. Since time is precious, I riffed on the classic and created this quick-cooking variation with seared boneless chicken and a pan sauce.

THIS SAUCE ALSO GOES WELL WITH: pork chops, turkey scaloppini, split Cornish game hens, portobello mushroom caps, and halibut fillets (refer to the tables on pages 208–26 for cooking tips).

**YIELD: 2 LARGE OR
4 MODERATE SERVINGS**

1 to 1½ pounds (450 to 675 g)
   boneless, skinless chicken breasts
   (2), sliced and pounded into
   cutlets (see page 87), or boneless,
   skinless chicken thighs (4 to 6),
   trimmed and pounded to an even
   thickness of ½ inch/1.25 cm
Salt and finely ground black pepper
2 to 3 tablespoons all-purpose
   flour for dredging (optional)
2 to 3 tablespoons clarified
   butter or neutral oil
2 tablespoons minced shallots
½ cup diced peeled tomato (drained
   canned diced tomatoes are fine)
¼ cup tarragon or red wine vinegar
1 cup low-sodium chicken stock,
   preferably homemade
1½ teaspoons chopped fresh tarragon
   or ½ teaspoon dried tarragon
3 to 4 tablespoons heavy cream
1 tablespoon chopped fresh parsley

PREP

Pat the chicken dry and season generously with salt and pepper. Dredge in the flour, if using, and pat off the excess.

SEAR

Heat a large skillet over medium-high heat. When it is hot, swirl in enough clarified butter to coat the bottom. Arrange the chicken in the pan so the pieces are evenly spaced. They should sizzle the moment they touch the hot oil. (If there is not enough room in the pan for all of the pieces, cook them in batches, wiping the pan clean and starting with fresh oil as needed.) Brown the chicken on the first side, about 3 minutes, then flip, reduce the heat slightly, and brown on the other side. The chicken does not need to be completely cooked through at this point. Transfer the chicken to a clean platter and keep warm while you make the sauce.

SAUCE

Discard the cooking fat and analyze the pan residue. Remove any unappealing bits or scorched flour. Cool the pan slightly, then return it to medium heat and swirl in the remaining clarified butter. Sauté the shallots until soft and golden brown, about 2 minutes. Add the tomatoes and cook until most of the juices have evaporated, about 1 minute. Deglaze the pan with the vinegar, being careful not to breathe in the fumes, or they may make you cough. Simmer until the vinegar is almost completely evaporated. Add the stock and tarragon and season with a pinch more each of salt and pepper.

Return the chicken and any collected juices to the pan and simmer until the chicken is cooked through and the sauce has thickened to the consistency of a thick gravy, about 4 minutes for chicken breast cutlets, 6 to 8 minutes for chicken thighs. Lift the chicken from the pan onto a clean platter or individual plates.

Stir the cream into the sauce and simmer until it is well blended and clings to the back of a spoon. Taste and adjust the seasoning with salt, pepper, and/or vinegar if needed.

Spoon the sauce over the chicken, sprinkle with the parsley, and serve.

Ingredients for Roasted Peanuts and Chile Oil: scallions, chiles, peanuts, and garlic

Chicken with Roasted Peanuts and Chile Oil

Garlic, chiles, and roasted peanuts are stirred together in the searing pan and bound with a bit of the deglazing liquid and good-quality oil. Nothing could be simpler. Look for a peanut oil that tastes and smells like peanuts. Lion & Globe brand is my favorite. Shaoxing is a Chinese wine similar to medium sherry. It has a good shelf life and is something I urge you to keep on hand.

THIS SAUCE ALSO GOES WELL WITH: tofu, snapper, flatiron steak, eggplant, broccoli, and tomato halves (refer to the tables on pages 208–26 for cooking tips).

YIELD: 2 LARGE OR 4 MODERATE SERVINGS

1 to 1½ pounds (450 to 675 g) boneless, skinless chicken thighs (4 to 6), trimmed, flattened, and pounded to an even thickness of ½ inch/ 1.25 cm, or boneless, skinless chicken breast cutlets

Salt and finely ground black or white pepper

¼ cup good-quality peanut oil

4 cloves garlic, sliced

2 to 3 Thai bird chiles or similar spicy chiles, thinly sliced, or ½ teaspoon red chile flakes, or to taste

⅓ cup coarsely chopped unsalted roasted peanuts

3 tablespoons Shaoxing wine or medium-dry sherry

1 tablespoon soy sauce

¼ cup sliced scallion greens

PREP

Pat the chicken dry and season generously with salt and pepper.

SEAR

Heat a large skillet over medium-high heat. When it is hot, swirl in enough oil to coat the bottom. Arrange the chicken in the pan so the pieces are evenly spaced. They should sizzle the moment they touch the hot oil. (If there is not enough room for all of the pieces, cook them in batches, wiping the pan clean and starting with fresh oil as needed.) Brown the chicken on the first side, 3 to 4 minutes. Flip, reduce the heat slightly, and brown the other side. Then continue to cook, flipping often, until the chicken is just cooked through, about 8 minutes more. Transfer the chicken to a platter or individual plates and keep warm while you make the sauce.

SAUCE

Discard the cooking oil and cool the pan slightly. Analyze the pan residue and remove any unappealing bits. Add the remaining oil, then add the garlic and chiles and stir until aromatic but not browned, about 20 seconds. Add the wine and soy sauce and use a wooden spoon to dissolve any brown residue on the bottom of the pan. Add the peanuts and scallion greens and stir to mix. Taste and adjust the seasoning with salt and pepper.

Spoon the sauce over the chicken and serve.

Chicken Breast Tenderloins with Agrodolce, Pine Nuts, and Golden Raisins

Agrodolce is an Italian sweet-and-sour sauce made with caramelized sugar and vinegar. Dried fruit and pine nuts are very commonly served in agrodolce. Fresh rosemary adds a welcome boost of perfume. Be sure to remove the skillet from the heat before you add the sugar, so you can monitor it—it can burn very quickly. This recipe makes a small amount of intensely flavored sauce. If you want more volume, you can always add a little butter at the end or drizzle the finished dish with good olive oil.

THIS SAUCE ALSO GOES WELL WITH: chicken or turkey scaloppini, boneless pork chops, calamari steaks, and broccoli (refer to the tables on pages 208–26 for cooking tips).

YIELD: 2 SERVINGS

10 to 12 ounces (285 to 340 g) chicken breast tenderloins (about 8)

Salt and freshly ground black pepper

About 1 tablespoon olive oil

1 tablespoon granulated sugar

3 tablespoons red wine vinegar

2 tablespoons pine nuts

2 tablespoons golden raisins, coarsely chopped

1 teaspoon chopped fresh rosemary

PREP

Because this recipe cooks so quickly, it is especially important to have all of the ingredients measured and within reach before you start to cook.

Pat the chicken tenders dry and season generously with salt and pepper.

SEAR

Heat a large skillet over medium-high heat. When it is hot, swirl in enough oil to coat the bottom. Arrange the chicken in the pan so the pieces are evenly spaced. They should sizzle the moment they touch the hot oil. (If there is not enough room in the pan for all of the pieces, cook them in batches, wiping the pan clean and starting with fresh oil as needed.) Brown the chicken on the first side, about 3 minutes. Flip, reduce the heat slightly, and brown on the other side. Then continue to cook and flip regularly until the chicken is just cooked through, about 4 minutes more.

SAUCE

Remove the pan from the burner, sprinkle the sugar around the chicken pieces in a thin, even layer, and return the pan to the heat. Within seconds, the sugar will melt, bubble, and start to caramelize. Quickly deglaze the pan with the vinegar, being careful to avoid breathing the fumes, or they may make you cough. Use the chicken pieces to gently loosen the brown residue and dissolve the caramelized sugar into the vinegar. There will be very little sauce. If you think it has become too reduced or concentrated, add a bit of water to return it to a thin, clinging glaze.

Stir in the pine nuts, raisins, and rosemary. Flip the pieces of chicken in the syrup until they are well coated. Taste and adjust the seasoning with plenty of salt and pepper.

Lift the chicken onto a clean platter or individual plates, drizzle with the sauce, and serve.

Chicken with Olive and Anchovy Oil

This quick-to-fix salty, savory oil complements many different foods, but I particularly like it crafted on a baseline of umami-rich chicken fond. Chicken thigh meat, rather than breasts, is a good choice here because the softer texture and richer taste stands up well to the strong flavors of the sauce. Olives and anchovies are both very salty, so watch your seasoning. Any good cured olives will work; pimento-stuffed olives will add color. Chopped fresh parsley is always welcome, if you have some on hand.

THIS SAUCE ALSO GOES WELL WITH: steaks, calamari steaks, polenta cakes, eggplant, and rustic bread slices (refer to the tables on pages 208–26 for cooking tips).

YIELD: 2 LARGE OR 4 MODERATE SERVINGS

1 to 1½ pounds (450 to 675g) boneless, skinless chicken thighs (4 to 6), pounded to an even thickness of ½ inch/1.25 cm

Salt and finely ground black pepper

1 to 2 tablespoons olive or neutral oil

4 to 6 cloves garlic, chopped

¼ teaspoon red chile flakes, or to taste

2 tablespoons red wine vinegar

¼ cup dry white wine, such as Sauvignon Blanc or Pinot Gris, or extra-dry vermouth

3 tablespoons pitted and chopped cured olives (6 to 8 medium), such as stuffed green, Kalamata, Gaeta, and/or Picholine

2 to 4 anchovy fillets, chopped, or to taste

> *continues on next page*

PREP

Pat the chicken thighs dry and season lightly with salt and pepper.

SEAR

Heat a large skillet over medium-high heat. When it is hot, swirl in just enough oil to coat the bottom. Arrange the chicken in the pan so the pieces are evenly spaced. They should sizzle the moment they touch the hot oil. (If there is not enough room in the pan for all of the pieces, cook them in batches, wiping the pan clean and starting with fresh oil if the residue seems burnt.) Sear the chicken until it is browned on the first side, about 3 minutes. Flip the chicken, reduce the heat slightly, and brown the other side. Then continue to cook, flipping often, until the chicken is just cooked through, about 8 minutes more. Transfer the chicken to a clean platter or plates and keep warm while you make the sauce.

1 teaspoon chopped fresh
    rosemary or ½ teaspoon
    crumbled dried rosemary
2 tablespoons chopped fresh parsley
3 to 4 tablespoons extra-virgin olive oil

SAUCE

Discard the cooking oil and analyze the pan residue. Remove any unappealing bits. Cool the pan slightly, then return it to medium heat and add a little oil if it seems dry. Add the garlic and chile flakes and sauté for about 20 seconds, until the aroma of the garlic has bloomed but it has not browned. Deglaze the pan with the vinegar, being careful not to breathe the fumes, or they may make you cough. Use a wooden spoon to dissolve any brown residue on the bottom of the pan. Add the wine and simmer until the pan is nearly dry. Stir in the olives, anchovies, rosemary, and parsley. Add enough extra-virgin olive oil to make a fluid sauce and gently heat until the flavors are thoroughly infused into the oil, about 2 minutes. Taste and adjust the seasoning. The anchovies and olives are very salty, so you may not need extra salt, but do add plenty of pepper.

Spoon the sauce over the chicken and serve.

Chicken "con Queso" (with Spicy Cheese Sauce)

This gooey, chile-laced cheese sauce was inspired by the famous Texas chip dip. The volume of sauce is far larger than that of most of my recipes, because you'll want to scoop it up with a heap of tortilla chips. This is a hybrid of a classic pan sauce and a roux-thickened cheese sauce. Rather than deglazing the pan, I make a light roux to pick up the pan residue. When you add the cheese, be sure to cook it only to the melting point, or it can turn gritty or start to separate. The cream cheese adds silkiness and helps keep the sauce smooth.

THIS SAUCE ALSO GOES WELL WITH: pork chops, meatballs or patties, and broccoli (refer to the tables on pages 208–26 for cooking tips).

**YIELD: 2 LARGE OR
4 MODERATE SERVINGS**

1 to 1½ pounds (450 to 675 g)
  boneless, skinless chicken
  breasts (2), sliced and pounded
  into cutlets (see page 87), or
  boneless, skinless chicken thighs
  (4 to 6), trimmed, flattened,
  and pounded to an even
  thickness of ½ inch/1.25 cm
Salt and freshly ground black pepper
2 to 3 tablespoons all-purpose
  flour for dredging (optional),
  plus 1 tablespoon flour
¼ cup clarified butter or neutral oil
⅓ cup minced yellow or white onion
3 tablespoons minced fresh chiles,
  such as green and red jalapeños,
  serranos, or Fresno, or to taste
2 cloves garlic, minced
1 teaspoon ground cumin

> continues on next page

PREP

Pat the chicken dry and season generously with salt and pepper. Dredge the chicken in the flour, if using, and pat off the excess.

SEAR

Heat a large skillet over medium-high heat. When it is hot, swirl in enough clarified butter to lightly coat the bottom. Arrange the chicken in the pan so the pieces are evenly spaced. They should sizzle the moment they touch the hot butter. (If there is not enough room in the pan for all of the pieces, cook them in batches, wiping the pan clean and starting with fresh butter as needed.) Brown the chicken on the first side, about 3 minutes. Flip, reduce the heat slightly, and brown on the other side. Then continue to cook, flipping often, until the chicken is just cooked through, 4 to 5 minutes more for breast cutlets, 6 to 8 minutes for thighs. Transfer the chicken to a clean platter or plates and keep warm while you make the sauce.

1 teaspoon pure chile powder,
   such as chipotle or New
   Mexico, or cayenne pepper

½ teaspoon paprika

1¼ cups low-sodium chicken
   stock, preferably homemade

2 ounces (60 g) cream cheese

4 ounces (115 g) sharp
   Cheddar cheese, grated

4 to 5 dashes hot chile sauce, such
   as Tabasco or Tapatío, or to taste

Additional chicken stock
   or milk (optional)

⅓ cup finely diced tomato

2 to 3 tablespoons thinly
   sliced scallion greens

Tortilla chips for serving

SAUCE

Discard the cooking oil and analyze the pan residue. Remove any unappealing bits or burnt flour. Cool the pan slightly, then return it to medium heat. Add the remaining butter and sauté the onions and chiles until tender, about 2 minutes. Add the garlic and cook for 20 seconds, until the aroma has bloomed but it hasn't browned.

Remove the pan from the heat, sprinkle in the 1 tablespoon flour, and stir until there are no lumps. Return the pan to the heat and cook, stirring constantly, until the flour is bubbly and just turning a golden color. Add the cumin, chile powder, and paprika, then add the stock and stir until evenly blended. Simmer until the sauce is the consistency of thin gravy, with no taste of raw flour, about 4 minutes.

Whisk the cream cheese into the sauce until melted and smooth. Remove the pan from the heat, add the Cheddar, and stir to melt; reheat the sauce if necessary, but do not let it boil once the cheese has been added. Taste and adjust the seasoning with salt, pepper, and hot sauce as desired. This sauce is quite thick; if you want it thinner, stir in some chicken stock or milk.

Spoon enough sauce over the chicken to moisten it evenly, and serve the remainder alongside. Garnish the chicken with the diced tomatoes and sliced scallions and serve with plenty of tortilla chips.

Chicken Legs with Sweet-and-Spicy Korean Chile Sauce

I find few dishes as comforting on a cold day as Korean *dukbokki*, chewy rice cakes bathed in sweet-and-spicy chile sauce. My friends and family love the sauce, but they aren't quite as enamored of the rice cakes, so I have adapted the recipe for chicken legs. *Gochujang*, the Korean fermented chile paste, has become very popular recently. I've found it in good supermarkets as well as Asian and specialty food stores. (I love the stuff so much that I actually fermented a crock of my own *gochujang*. It's divine!) Unlike many pan sauces, this holds remarkably well, and the dish can even be made ahead of time.

THIS SAUCE ALSO GOES WELL WITH: pork chops, cross-cut beef short ribs, tofu, sweet potato planks, and fish cakes (refer to the tables on pages 208–26 for cooking tips).

YIELD: 4 SERVINGS

6 to 8 chicken legs (drumsticks; about 2 pounds/900 g)

Salt and freshly ground black or white pepper

3 to 4 tablespoons peanut or neutral oil

1 medium yellow onion, thinly sliced (2 cups)

3 cloves garlic, minced

1½ cups low-sodium chicken stock, preferably homemade

¼ cup *gochujang* (Korean fermented chile paste), or to taste

¼ cup brown rice syrup, honey, or granulated sugar, or to taste

1 teaspoon toasted sesame oil

2 scallions, thinly sliced

PREP

Pat the chicken dry and season generously with salt and pepper.

SEAR

Heat a large skillet over medium-high heat. When it is hot, swirl in enough oil to coat the bottom. Arrange the chicken in the pan so the pieces are evenly spaced. They should sizzle the moment they touch the hot oil. Gradually brown the legs, turning occasionally, on all sides. Do not dig or scrape at the pieces if they seem to be sticking, just leave them to cook longer, and they will eventually release themselves. When the chicken legs are evenly browned, transfer them to a clean plate or platter. (They will not be fully cooked at this point.)

SAUCE

Discard the frying oil and analyze the pan residue. Brown, crispy bits of skin and meat are fine; they will soften in the sauce as it cooks. If the fond looks or smells burnt, rinse the pan clean and wipe dry. Return the skillet to medium heat and add a thin layer of fresh oil. Add the onions and sauté until soft and golden brown. Add the garlic and cook for 20 seconds. Deglaze the pan with the chicken stock and use a wooden spoon to loosen and dissolve any residue in the bottom of the skillet. Stir in the *gochujang* and rice syrup.

Return the chicken to the pan and turn the pieces so they are well coated. Bring to a boil, then reduce to a gentle simmer and partially cover with a lid, setting it askew so some of the liquid will evaporate as the chicken cooks. Simmer, flipping the pieces now and then, until the chicken is fully cooked, about 20 minutes. (The USDA recommends that chicken be cooked to an internal temperature of 165°F/74°C, but for succulent dark meat, I recommend you cook it to an internal temperature of 170° to 180°F/77° to 82°C). Lift the chicken legs onto a clean platter.

Increase the temperature and boil the sauce, uncovered, stirring often to prevent burning, until it has thickened and become slightly sticky. Taste and adjust the seasoning with salt, chile paste, and/or rice syrup if desired.

Spoon enough sauce over the chicken to cover; serve the rest alongside. Drizzle the chicken with the sesame oil, garnish with the scallions, and serve.

Tamarind-Glazed Chicken Heaped with Fresh Mint and Cilantro

Tamarind-Glazed Chicken
Heaped with Fresh Mint and Cilantro

Many years ago I fell in love with *asam ayam*, an Indonesian chicken and tamarind stew. This quick reduction-style pan sauce combines some of the same flavors: naturally sweet and tangy tamarind, fragrant ground coriander, and fresh herbs to finish. Tamarind is sold in many forms. I buy mine in bricks at Asian markets because it is a little tangier and I like the balance of sweetness and acidity, and it also stores well at room temperature. To use it, I pull off lumps, mash and knead them in warm water, and then pass it all through a sieve. Tamarind can also be found as large brown pods with fragile hulls, sold in the produce section of some specialty markets. To access the pulp, break away the exterior, then remove the fibers and seeds before soaking. If you prefer to buy ready-to-use tamarind puree, try Garden Queen brand. It isn't quite as flavorful, but I think it is the closest substitute to freshly soaked pulp.

THIS SAUCE ALSO GOES WELL WITH: rockfish, thin pork chops, duck breast, shrimp, and tofu (refer to the tables on pages 208–26 for cooking tips).

**YIELD: 2 LARGE OR
4 MODERATE SERVINGS**

3 heaping tablespoons lump
    tamarind (or substitute about
    ⅓ cup commercial tamarind
    puree, such as Garden Queen
    brand; see headnote)
1½ cups warm water
1 to 1½ pounds (450 to 675 g)
    boneless, skinless chicken thighs
    (4 to 6), trimmed, flattened, and
    pounded to an even thickness
    of ½ inch/1.25 cm, or boneless,
    skinless chicken breast cutlets
Salt and freshly ground
    black or white pepper

> *continues on next page*

PREP

Put the tamarind and water in a small saucepan and bring to a boil. Stir well, remove from the heat, and leave the tamarind to soften for about 5 minutes.

When it is cool enough to touch, use your fingers to knead and loosen the tamarind pulp from the fibers and seeds. Press the mixture through a sieve set over a bowl; discard any dry, fibrous material. You should end up with about ¾ cup brown sweet-and-sour liquid with a slightly pulpy texture.

Or, if you are using commercially prepared tamarind pulp, omit the soaking step and just add enough water to make ¾ cup. The liquid should be piquant but not overly sour, so adjust it accordingly.

Pat the chicken dry and season generously with salt and pepper.

> *continues on next page*

About 2 tablespoons peanut,
  coconut, or neutral oil

2 teaspoons minced fresh ginger

¼ teaspoon red chile
  flakes, or to taste

2 teaspoons ground coriander

1 tablespoon brown sugar
  or grated palm sugar

¼ cup coarsely chopped
  fresh cilantro

¼ cup coarsely chopped fresh mint

1 tablespoon sliced scallion greens

SEAR

Heat a large skillet over medium-high heat. When it is hot, swirl in enough oil to coat the bottom. Arrange the chicken in the pan so the pieces are evenly spaced. They should sizzle the moment they touch the hot oil. (If there is not enough room in the pan for all of the pieces, cook them in batches, wiping the pan clean and starting with fresh oil as needed.) Brown the chicken on the first side, about 3 minutes, then flip, reduce the heat slightly, and brown the other side. Then continue to cook and flip until the chicken is just cooked through, about 8 minutes. Transfer the chicken to a clean platter and keep warm while you make the sauce.

SAUCE

Discard the cooking oil and cool the pan slightly, then analyze the pan residue and remove any unappealing bits. Return the skillet to medium heat and add some fresh oil if the pan is very dry. Add the ginger and chile flakes and cook for about 20 seconds, until the aroma of the ginger has bloomed but it has not browned. Add the ground coriander and stir to mix, then stir in the tamarind liquid and brown sugar. Use a wooden spoon to help dissolve any residue on the bottom of the pan.

Return the chicken and any juices to the pan and simmer, flipping often, until the sauce is concentrated and clings to the chicken, 2 to 3 minutes. Taste and adjust the seasoning with salt and pepper as needed.

Lift the chicken onto a clean platter or individual plates. Spoon the sauce over, heap with the cilantro, mint, and scallions, and serve.

Turkey Scaloppini with Brown Butter and Crispy Sage

This recipe has only three fundamental ingredients: turkey, butter, and sage. Because it is so elementary, I decided that it was the perfect recipe to put my skillet biases to the test. I made two separate batches, one in a stainless steel skillet and the other in a nonstick pan. In the end, both recipes looked nearly identical, but the turkey cooked in the "sticky," untreated pan tasted far better. The fond that developed added loads of savory flavor and the lighter pan interior helped me judge when the butter had reached the perfect brown. It showed me once again how the simplest of recipes can be elevated to great heights with good technique, tools, and ingredients.

THIS SAUCE ALSO GOES WELL WITH: pork or chicken scaloppini, salmon, sole, sweet potato planks, and polenta cakes (refer to the tables on pages 208–26 for cooking tips).

YIELD: 3 OR 4 SERVINGS

1 small skin-on, bone-in turkey breast (about 2 pounds/900 g)

Salt and freshly ground black or white pepper

2 to 3 tablespoons all-purpose or rice flour for dredging (optional)

About 1 tablespoon clarified butter or neutral oil

2 tablespoons unsalted butter

8 to 10 small fresh sage leaves, slivered or torn (about 2 tablespoons)

PREP

To make the turkey scaloppini, remove the skin and bones. Slice the turkey breast across the grain on a slight bias into pieces about ⅜ inch/1 cm thick. Pound these into very thin cutlets as you would chicken (see page 87). Pat the turkey dry and season generously with salt and pepper. Dredge the scaloppini in the flour, if using, and pat off the excess.

SEAR

Heat a large sauté pan over medium-high heat. When it is hot, add just enough clarified butter to coat the bottom evenly. You will need to cook the turkey in batches, wiping the pan clean and starting with fresh oil as needed. Arrange a few of the scaloppini in the pan so the pieces are evenly spaced. They should sizzle the moment they touch the hot butter. Sear the scaloppini until browned on the first side, about 3 minutes, then flip, reduce the temperature slightly, and continue to cook, flipping regularly, until the turkey is just cooked through, about 4 minutes. Transfer the turkey to a clean platter and keep warm while you cook the remaining batches and then make the sauce.

> *continues on next page*

SAUCE

Discard the frying fat and analyze the pan residue. Remove any unappealing bits or scorched flour. Cool the pan slightly, then return it to medium heat. Add the 2 tablespoons whole butter and the sage. As the butter melts, use a wooden spoon to rub the bottom of the pan and dislodge as much residue as possible; because there is no water in this recipe, the residue will not dissolve as it would with wine or another deglazing liquid, but it can be loosened to flavor the sauce. Cook until the butter solids are the color of a brown paper bag and the sage is crispy, about 1½ minutes. When the crackling and foam subside and the moisture from the sage has evaporated, the temperature will rise and the butter will brown quickly.

Immediately pour the sauce over the turkey. Season with salt and pepper and serve.

Turkey Scaloppini with Brown Butter and
Crispy Sage (page 111)

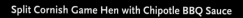
Split Cornish Game Hen with Chipotle BBQ Sauce

Split Cornish Game Hen
with Chipotle BBQ Sauce

Every time I make Cornish hens, I wonder why I don't cook them more often. They are easy to find, reasonably priced, and perfect to share. Splitting them in half makes them easier to handle and reduces the cooking time. Instructions are included below, but your butcher might be willing to do that for you. This recipe has what I consider to be a "user friendly" level of chipotle; if you want it spicier and smokier, double it. I often do. If you want to double the recipe, two split hens will fit in a large cast-iron skillet, but the sauce will have to be stretched.

THIS SAUCE ALSO GOES WELL WITH: chicken pieces, pork chops, sausages, and meatballs or patties (refer to the tables on pages 208–26 for cooking tips).

**YIELD: 1 LARGE OR
2 MODERATE SERVINGS**

1 Cornish game hen
   (1½ pounds/675 g)
Salt and finely ground black pepper
About 2 tablespoons neutral
   oil or clarified butter
2 tablespoons minced onion or shallot
1 to 2 cloves garlic, minced
1 tablespoon minced chipotle
   chile in adobo, or to taste
½ teaspoon paprika
3 tablespoons apple cider
   vinegar or red wine vinegar
½ cup ketchup
3 tablespoons granulated sugar,
   brown sugar, or honey
2 tablespoons Worcestershire sauce

PREP

Heat the oven to 425°F/220°C.

Cut the hen in half: The easiest way to do this is to use shears to cut down along each side of the backbone and remove it. With the breast side down, press on it to flatten it, then use a sharp knife to cut through the cartilage at the sternum and split the bird evenly into 2 portions. Snip off the wings to leave only the "drumette" portion, so the halves will brown more evenly. Pat the hen dry and season generously on both sides with salt and pepper.

SEAR

Heat a large ovenproof skillet over medium-high heat. When it is hot, swirl in just enough oil to coat the bottom. Place the game hen pieces skin side down in the skillet. They should sizzle the moment they touch the hot oil. Sear the pieces, rolling them and propping them up slightly as necessary, until the skin is well browned, about 6 minutes.

> continues on next page

Flip the pieces and put the skillet in the oven. Pan-roast the hen for 6 minutes, then turn the pieces skin side down and cook for another 4 to 5 minutes. Flip again and continue to cook until the thickest part of the thigh reaches an internal temperature of at least 165°F/74°C; cooking the hen through will take a total of about 18 to 20 minutes of roasting.

The pan handle will be very hot, so be sure to use an oven mitt from this point on. Lift the pieces from the skillet onto a clean platter and keep warm while you make the sauce.

SAUCE

Analyze the pan contents. If the juices and residue smell good and are an appealing color, keep them. If not, discard them and wipe the pan clean. Return the skillet to medium heat and swirl in a bit more oil if it is dry. Sauté the onions until soft, 1 to 2 minutes. Add the garlic and cook for another 20 seconds. Stir in the chipotle and paprika and deglaze the pan with the vinegar, being careful not to breathe the fumes, or they may make you cough. Use a wooden spoon to loosen and dissolve any brown residue on the bottom of the pan. Stir in the ketchup, sugar, Worcestershire sauce, and any juices that have collected on the platter with the game hens. Bring the sauce to a simmer and let cook for about 2 minutes, until the flavors blend but the consistency is still quite thin. Taste and adjust the seasoning as you like with salt, pepper, chiles, sugar, and/or vinegar.

Return the game hen halves to the skillet and simmer, flipping the pieces until they have a slightly sticky coating of sauce. Transfer the pieces to the platter and pour the remaining sauce over the top, or serve alongside. Serve immediately.

Duck Breasts with Blackberry and Port Demi-Glace

A bite of perfectly cooked duck breast with a gloss of flavorful pan sauce is a glorious thing. There's only one drawback—once you master this recipe, the luster of fine-dining restaurants can fade. It's tough to pay steakhouse prices when your home-cooked meals are superior.

A duck breast has a thick layer of fat between the succulent meat and the skin. Cutting slashes in the duck skin helps to render out the fat as the duck cooks. Chilling just the meaty side of the breasts keeps the duck meat pink while the skin side becomes fully cooked and crisped.

While the USDA recommends that all poultry be cooked to 160° to 170°F/71° to 76°C, many chefs prefer red-meat birds cooked to medium-rare, about 133°F/56°C. There is no absolute guarantee that it will be safe, but the improved flavor and texture make it worth the risk for me.

Don't pour the sauce over the duck. Instead, spoon it onto the plates and arrange the sliced duck on top; otherwise, the skin that you so carefully crisped will become soggy.

THIS SAUCE ALSO GOES WILL WITH: pork tenderloin, semi-boneless quail, game meats, and wild salmon (refer to the tables on pages 208–26 for cooking tips).

YIELD: 2 TO 4 SERVINGS

2 to 4 large boneless duck breasts
   (6 to 8 ounces/170 to 225 g each)
2 cups (about 12 ounces/340 g)
   fresh or frozen blackberries
1 to 2 tablespoons neutral oil
1 tablespoon finely minced shallot
1 cup port
1 tablespoon duck, veal, or chicken
   demi-glace base, such as More
   than Gourmet brand, or homemade
   glace de viande, if available
2 tablespoons cold unsalted butter,
   cut into pats or small cubes
Salt and freshly ground black pepper

PREP

Heat the oven to 450°F/230°C.

To help ensure that the meat remains pink, place the duck breasts skin side up on zip-top bags of ice or ice packs for 5 to 7 minutes. This chills the meat while the skin and fat start to warm to room temperature. (If you prefer duck breasts cooked more well-done, you can omit this step.)

While the duck is chilling, if using fresh blackberries, select 8 to 12 of the prettiest berries and set them aside for garnish. Mash or puree the rest of the berries (or all of the frozen berries) and press the pulp through a sieve into a bowl to make approximately ⅔ cup juice.

Use a sharp knife to score the duck skin in lines about ½ inch/1 cm apart, then repeat in the other direction to form a crisscross pattern. This will help render out more of the fat. Do not salt the skin; the moisture that is drawn out makes browning and crisping the skin more challenging.

> *continues on next page*

SEAR

Heat a large ovenproof skillet over medium-high heat. When it is hot, swirl in just enough oil to coat the bottom. Place the duck breasts skin side down in the skillet. They should sizzle the moment they touch the hot oil. Sear until the skin is dark brown and crisp, 4 to 5 minutes. The breasts will shrink quite dramatically as they cook.

Flip the breasts and put the skillet in the oven. Pan-roast the duck, flipping the breasts every 2 minutes to ensure even cooking, until the thickest part of the breast just starts to spring back when you press on it; at this point, the meat should be medium-rare (with an internal temperature of 130° to 135°F/54° to 57°C). It will continue to cook through a bit as it rests.

The pan handle will be very hot, so be sure to use an oven mitt from this point on. Transfer the duck to a carving board. Do not cover it, or the skin will soften.

SAUCE

Pour out all but a thin film of the hot duck fat. (Save the fat; it can be strained and is great for frying potatoes.) Sauté the shallots until softened and aromatic, about 30 seconds. Deglaze the pan with the port, using a wooden spoon to dissolve any brown bits and residue on the bottom of the pan. Bring the port to a full boil and reduce the volume by half. Add the demi-glace and stir to melt completely. Stir in the blackberry juice and pulp and simmer until the sauce is the consistency of a thin, slightly sticky gravy. Gradually stir in the butter, one piece at a time, until just melted. Taste and adjust the seasoning with salt and pepper.

If the duck feels cool or the skin has become soft, pop it back in the oven for a minute or two, or crisp it up with a kitchen torch. Slice each duck breast on the bias into 4 or 5 pieces and sprinkle with a touch of salt. Spoon the sauce onto plates, top with the fanned duck slices, and garnish with the fresh blackberries, if you have them. Serve immediately.

Duck Breasts with Blackberry and
Port Demi-Glace (page 117),
served with roasted potatoes

MEATS

Rib Steak with Simple Red Wine and Herb Sauce

Steak with Simple Red Wine and Herb Sauce

Red wine sauce is something I am often asked about. In most cases, people want to duplicate the complex wine-spiked meat reductions they have enjoyed at restaurants. Once I explain that those sauces take at least three days to make from scratch, they are far more receptive to this recipe, a simple pan sauce that can be whipped up in minutes. This is essentially a Wine-From-Your-Glass pan sauce (see page 206), but I have added the option of stirring in a touch of commercial demi-glace for cooks who don't mind "cheating" a little to get a more savory, intense flavor.

Don't fall for the temptation of tucking away bottles of unpleasant wines "for cooking." Bad wine doesn't magically get better in a skillet. It's fine, though, to use up a decent bottle that was opened a few days earlier.

THIS SAUCE ALSO GOES WELL WITH: lamb chops, buffalo steaks, duck breasts, and portobello mushroom caps (refer to the tables on pages 208–26 for cooking tips).

YIELD: 2 LARGE OR 4 MODERATE SERVINGS

1 to 1½ pounds (450 to 675 g) steak(s) of your choice, such as NY strip, rib steak, sirloin, or flatiron

Salt and freshly ground black pepper

About 2 tablespoons clarified butter or neutral oil

2 tablespoons minced shallots or onion

1 clove garlic, minced

½ cup robust red wine, such as Merlot, Syrah, or Cabernet Sauvignon, preferably unoaked

1 to 2 teaspoons demi-glace base, such as More than Gourmet brand, or *glace de viande*, if available (optional)

2 tablespoons cold unsalted butter, cut into pats or small cubes

1 tablespoon chopped fresh herbs, such as parsley, tarragon, chives, or rosemary

PREP

Pat the steak(s) dry and season generously with salt and pepper.

SEAR

Heat a large skillet over medium-high heat. When it is hot, swirl in enough clarified butter to coat the bottom. Arrange the meat in the pan; if there is more than one steak, make sure they are evenly spaced. They should sizzle the moment they touch the hot oil. Brown on the first side, about 3 minutes. Flip, reduce the heat slightly, and brown on the other side. Then continue to cook, flipping regularly, until the meat reaches your preferred doneness (see page 17). This may take only a minute for thin steaks and as long as 15 for thicker steaks cooked to well-done. Remember that the internal temperature will rise a degree or two after the meat is removed from the skillet. Transfer the steak to a clean platter and keep warm while you make the sauce. (It is always best to let meat rest for a few minutes after cooking so the internal juices will remain in the steak rather than flowing all over the plate when it is sliced.)

> *continues on next page*

SAUCE

Discard the cooking fat and cool the pan slightly, then analyze the pan residue and remove any unappealing bits. A very dark brown, sticky fond is fine; if the fond is black, crumbly, or flaky, wipe the pan clean before proceeding. Return the skillet to medium heat. Add some fresh clarified butter if the pan is very dry. Add the shallots and cook until softened, about 1 minute. Add the garlic and cook for 20 seconds more, or until the aroma has bloomed but it has not browned. Deglaze the pan with the red wine. Use a wooden spoon to dissolve the brown residue on the bottom of the pan, then increase the heat and simmer until the aroma of raw alcohol is cooked off. If you have chosen to use the demi-glace, add it now. When the wine has reduced to a few tablespoons, add the herbs, then gradually add the butter, a few pieces at a time, just until melted. Taste and adjust the seasoning with salt and pepper.

Spoon the wine and herb sauce over or alongside the steak and serve immediately.

Skirt Steaks with Artichoke and Pickled Pepper Relish

This antipasto-like relish can be as salty, tangy, or spicy as you like, depending on the pickled peppers you choose. If you are using whole pickled peppers, cut the stems off and squeeze out most of the seeds before chopping and measuring them. My personal favorites are Seattle's beloved Mama Lil's Original or "Kick Butt" goat horn peppers.

I like my skirt steak cooked longer than any other cut of beef. I think the edges are best crispy and brown. Sometimes I use the very thin *carne asada* slices at my local *carnicería*.

THIS SAUCE ALSO GOES WELL WITH: chicken, mackerel, tuna steaks, Italian sausages, and polenta cakes (refer to the tables on pages 208–26 for cooking tips).

YIELD: 2 OR 3 SERVINGS

¾ to 1 pound (340 to 450 g) skirt steaks

Salt and freshly ground black pepper

About 1 tablespoon neutral or olive oil

2 tablespoons minced onion

3 cloves garlic, chopped

¼ teaspoon red chile flakes, or to taste

3 tablespoons chopped frozen or drained marinated artichoke hearts

Scant ¼ cup stemmed, seeded, and coarsely chopped pickled cherry peppers, peperoncini, or pickled chile peppers

½ teaspoon dried oregano

1 tablespoon red wine vinegar

¼ cup extra-dry vermouth or dry white wine

1 cup baby spinach, chopped

3 to 4 tablespoons extra-virgin olive oil, or as needed

PREP

Pat the steaks dry and season generously with salt and pepper.

SEAR

Heat a large skillet over medium-high heat. When it is hot, swirl in enough oil to coat the bottom. Arrange the steaks in the pan so they are evenly spaced. They should sizzle the moment they touch the hot oil. (Do not overcrowd the pan; if necessary, cook the steaks in batches, wiping the pan clean and adding fresh oil as needed.) Sear the steaks until dark brown and crisp on the first side, 2 to 3 minutes. Flip, reduce the heat slightly, and brown on the other side, then continue to cook, flipping the steaks regularly, until they have reached your preferred doneness (see page 17). The steaks will continue to cook slightly as the meat rests. Transfer the steaks to a clean platter or individual plates, or to a carving board if you are going to slice them before serving.

> *continues on next page*

SAUCE

Discard the cooking oil and cool the pan slightly, then analyze the pan residue. A very dark brown, sticky fond is fine; if the fond is black, crumbly, or flaky, wipe the pan clean before proceeding. Return the skillet to medium heat and add a little fresh oil if the pan is very dry. Sauté the onions until tender and browned, about 2 minutes. Add the garlic and chile flakes and cook until the aroma blooms, about 20 seconds. Stir in the chopped artichokes, peppers, and oregano, then stir in the vinegar, being careful to avoid the fumes, or they may make you cough. Use a wooden spoon to dissolve any brown residue on the bottom of the pan. Add the vermouth, increase the temperature, and simmer until the raw aroma of alcohol is cooked off and the liquid has reduced by half.

Stir in the spinach until barely wilted, about 30 seconds. Finish with enough olive oil to make the mixture saucy and cohesive. Taste and adjust the seasoning with salt and pepper as needed.

Spoon the relish over the steaks, drizzle on additional olive oil if desired, and serve.

Skirt Steaks with Artichoke and Pickled Pepper Relish (page 125)

Petite Sirloin Steaks with Bacon, Balsamic Vinegar, and Basil

This is my nephew's favorite recipe. I roped him into this project early on, when I needed to observe how new cooks approached searing foods and making pan sauces. We prepped the ingredients together and talked through some techniques, then I handed him the recipe, stepped back, and watched him execute it perfectly. We both immediately saw potential not just in the book, but in his cooking prowess. Since then, he has made variations of this dish countless times for friends and family, with steaks ranging from cheap to exquisite. He makes me very proud. Don't use a fancy balsamic vinegar here. You want brightness and acidity. Mellow aged vinegars are best used as a finishing drizzle.

THIS SAUCE ALSO GOES WELL WITH: lamb chops or patties, pork, chicken, eggplant, and tomato halves (refer to the tables on pages 208–26 for cooking tips).

YIELD: 2 MODERATE OR 4 SMALL SERVINGS

1 to 1½ pounds (450 to 675 g) small sirloin steaks or steaks of your choice

Salt and freshly ground black pepper

About 1 tablespoon neutral or olive oil

¼ cup minced bacon or pancetta (about 1 thick-cut slice or 2 thin slices)

2 cloves garlic, chopped

¼ teaspoon red chile flakes, or to taste

3 tablespoons balsamic vinegar (see headnote), or to taste

¼ cup robust red wine, such as Merlot or Cabernet Sauvignon

2 tablespoons cold unsalted butter, cut into pats or small cubes (or substitute extra-virgin olive oil)

¼ cup chopped fresh basil

PREP

Pat the steaks dry and season generously with salt and pepper.

SEAR

Heat a large skillet over medium-high heat. When it is hot, swirl in enough oil to coat the bottom. Arrange the steaks in the skillet so they are evenly spaced. They should sizzle the moment they touch the hot oil. (If there is not enough room in the pan for all the steaks, cook them in batches, wiping the plan clean and starting with fresh oil as needed.) Sear until the steaks are well browned on the first side, then flip. If the steaks are very thin, they may be cooked to rare within a minute. If they are thicker or you prefer your steaks cooked more, reduce the temperature slightly and cook until they are slightly below your desired internal temperature (see page 17). They will continue to cook slightly as they rest. Transfer the steaks to a clean platter or individual plates and keep warm while you make the sauce.

SAUCE

Discard the oil and cool the pan slightly, then analyze the residue. A very dark brown, sticky fond is fine; if the fond is black, crumbly, or flaky, wipe the pan clean before proceeding. Return the skillet to medium heat and add the bacon. Add some oil if the bacon is lean. Cook the bacon until browned but not completely crisp. Add the garlic and chile flakes and cook until the aroma of the garlic blooms, about 20 seconds. Deglaze the pan with the vinegar, being careful to not breathe the fumes, as they may make you cough. The vinegar will evaporate quickly. Add the wine and use a wooden spoon to dissolve the brown bits on the bottom of the pan. Increase the temperature slightly and simmer until the aroma of raw alcohol has cooked away and the volume of liquid is reduced by half. If you are using butter, gradually stir it in, a few pieces at a time, just until it melts. Or stir in the olive oil. Taste the sauce and adjust the seasoning with salt and pepper as necessary. Add a few drops of vinegar for added sharpness if the taste seems sweet.

Spoon the sauce over the steaks, scatter on the basil, and serve.

BASTING STEAKS

Chefs sometimes spoon hot oil or butter over meats as they sizzle in a skillet. This helps cook both sides and can also help retain the natural juices. Using butter will saturate steaks with an intoxicating flavor and aroma. If you want to try basting, you need to start with far more fat than these recipes call for: ¼ cup or even more. Heat the skillet, add the fat, and sear the first side of the meat, then flip as usual. As the second side cooks, tilt the pan slightly so you can collect some of the hot oil or butter in a spoon, and pour it over the meat. Repeat this continuously until the steak is where you want it. Discard any overheated or "spent" oil (or butter) before moving on to the sauce-making steps. This technique works particularly well with "reverse seared" or sous-vide steaks (see page 141).

Flatiron Steak with Warm Green Vinaigrette

Italian salsa verde, Argentinean chimichurri, and Caribbean "green seasoning" are all bright, tangy fresh herb sauces that are traditionally served with beef. A while back, I was inspired to use some leftover "green sauce" as a pan sauce and was thrilled with how it picked up an extra layer of flavor from the savory residue while still remaining fresh tasting. Virtually any mix of fresh herbs can be used in this recipe, as long as there is a base of tender leaves. The vinaigrette can be made a day or two ahead and kept in the refrigerator; the colors will not be as vibrant, but the flavors will be more infused.

THIS SAUCE ALSO GOES WELL WITH: kielbasa, salmon, shrimp, calamari steaks, and portobello mushroom caps (refer to the tables on pages 208–26 for cooking tips).

YIELD: 2 OR 3 SERVINGS

One ¾- to 1-pound (340 to 450-g) flatiron steak, left whole or cut into portions
Salt and freshly ground black pepper
About 1 tablespoon neutral oil
2 tablespoons finely chopped onion
3 to 4 cloves garlic, chopped
¼ teaspoon red chile flakes, or to taste
¼ cup red wine vinegar
¼ cup chopped fresh parsley
3 tablespoons chopped mixed tender fresh herbs, such as basil, cilantro, dill, tarragon, chives, scallion greens, and/or chervil
1 tablespoon chopped "woody" or strong fresh herbs, such as rosemary, thyme, savory, and/or sage
¼ cup extra-virgin olive oil

PREP

Pat the steak dry and season generously with salt and pepper.

SEAR

Heat a large skillet over medium-high heat. When it is hot, swirl in enough oil to coat the bottom. Arrange the steak in the pan; if the steak has been cut into pieces, they should be evenly spaced. The steak should sizzle the moment it touches the hot oil. Sear it until it is dark brown on the first side, about 3 minutes. Flip, reduce the heat slightly, and brown the other side. Then continue to cook and flip regularly until the meat has reached your preferred doneness (see page 17). The steak will continue to cook slightly as it rests. Transfer the steak to a carving board or clean platter and keep warm while you make the sauce.

SAUCE

Discard the cooking oil and cool the pan slightly, then analyze the pan residue. A very dark brown, sticky fond is fine; if the fond is black, crumbly, or flaky, wipe the pan clean before proceeding. Return the skillet to medium heat and add a little fresh oil if it is very dry. Sauté the onions until tender and browned, about 2 minutes. Add the garlic and chile flakes and cook until the aroma blooms, about 20 seconds. Deglaze the pan with the vinegar, being careful not to breathe the fumes, or they may make you cough. Use a wooden spoon to dissolve any brown residue on the bottom of the pan.

Remove the pan from the heat, add the parsley, the other herbs, and the oil and warm through with the residual heat of the pan. Taste and adjust the seasoning with salt and pepper as needed.

Slice the steak on the bias. Arrange on a platter or individual plates and spoon enough sauce over the slices to moisten them. Serve with any remaining sauce alongside.

NY Strip Steak with Strong Mustard Gravy and Crispy Rye Crumbs, served with watercress

NY Strip Steak with Strong Mustard Gravy and Crispy Rye Crumbs

This recipe was borne from my love of roast beef sandwiches. The steak is seared until crisp on the outside but still pink in the middle and topped with a strong mustard sauce, thin rings of raw shallots, and a scattering of crispy, salty rye bread crumbs. My favorite local butcher sells NY strip steaks that weigh over a pound each, so I usually cook a single steak, slice it, and serve it family-style. I find it far more appealing to enjoy a few slices than to tackle a whopping-big steak of my own. Use good, pungent mustard. I stir up some Colman's while prepping the ingredients, but you can substitute your favorite extra-strong prepared mustard.

THIS SAUCE ALSO GOES WELL WITH: pork chops, lamb chops, duck breasts, calf's liver, chicken pieces, and bratwurst or smoked sausages (refer to the tables on pages 208–26 for cooking tips).

YIELD: 2 LARGE OR 4 MODERATE SERVINGS

3 slices stale rye bread

3 tablespoons olive oil or clarified butter, or as needed

Salt and freshly ground black pepper

1 clove garlic, finely minced or pressed

1 shallot, thinly sliced and separated into rings

1 to 1½ pounds (450 to 675 g) thick-cut (1-inch/2.5-cm or more) NY strip steak(s)

About 1 tablespoon neutral oil

¼ cup red wine vinegar

1 cup reduced-sodium beef stock, preferably homemade

1½ teaspoons cornstarch, stirred together with 1 tablespoon cold water until smooth

4 teaspoons Colman's English mustard powder, stirred together with cold water until smooth

1 tablespoon Worcestershire sauce

PREP

Heat the oven to 375°F/190°C.

Make the crispy rye crumbs: Remove and discard the crusts from the bread. Put the bread in the bowl of a food processor and pulse until chopped into coarse, even crumbs.

Line a plate with paper towels. Heat a large skillet over medium heat. When it is hot, swirl in the olive oil, add the bread crumbs, and fry, stirring constantly, until they start to smell toasted, 2 to 3 minutes. Add the garlic and cook, adding a bit more oil if necessary, until the crumbs are dry and crispy. Scatter the crumbs onto the paper towel–lined plate, season with salt and pepper, and set aside. (This can be done up to a day ahead.)

Cover the shallot rings with cold water in a small bowl and let soak while you prepare the steak and sauce. This helps to mellow their sharpness and crisp up the texture.

Pat the steak dry and season generously with salt and pepper.

> *continues on next page*

SEAR

Heat a large ovenproof sauté pan over medium-high heat. Swirl in just enough neutral oil to coat the bottom. Arrange the steak in the pan. It should sizzle the moment it touches the hot oil. Sear until dark brown on the first side, about 3 minutes.

Flip the steak and put the pan in the oven. Cook, flipping the meat every 2 to 3 minutes, until just a few degrees below your desired temperature (see page 17), about 7 minutes total for medium-rare. The internal temperature of the steak will rise a bit as it rests.

The pan handle will be very hot, so be sure to use an oven mitt from this point on. Transfer the steak to a carving board to rest while you make the sauce.

SAUCE

Discard the cooking oil and analyze the pan residue. Remove any unappealing bits or burnt residue. Deglaze the pan with the vinegar, being careful to avoid breathing the fumes, or they may make you cough. Use a wooden spoon to dissolve any flavorful residue on the bottom of the pan. Reduce the vinegar until it is nearly gone. Add the beef stock, bring to a boil, and reduce the volume by half. Stir the cornstarch mixture well, drizzle half of it into the sauce, and simmer until the gravy thickens slightly. I like my gravies quite thin. If you want a thicker gravy, add the remaining cornstarch mixture or continue to reduce the gravy until it reaches your desired consistency.

Stir a few spoonfuls of the hot gravy into the mustard until it is smooth and warm. Pour this mixture back into the pan and heat gently. Add the Worcestershire, then taste and adjust the seasoning with additional salt and pepper if needed.

Slice the steak on the bias and arrange on a platter or individual plates. Spoon enough gravy over the slices to moisten them evenly. Scatter the crumbs over and top with the drained crisp shallot rings. Serve with any remaining gravy alongside.

Steak Diane

Steak Diane is a classic seared and sauced entrée. Some restaurants still prepare it tableside, claiming theirs to be the best or most authentic recipe. The dish is usually made with beef tenderloin, shallots, flambéed Cognac, and lots of butter. Sometimes mushrooms, Dijon mustard, a splash of Worcestershire and cream are added, but there is no one "true" version. The classic Escoffier recipe for sauce Diane suggests the sauce be finished with whipped cream and shaved truffles. James Beard's recipe calls for half a pound of butter and half a cup of Armagnac. (No wonder classic pan sauces were considered special-occasion decadences.)

The dish's adaptability means that there are a lot of different opinions on the proper way to make Steak Diane. So I decided to create a recipe that can be adapted to personal taste and circumstance. I have included the most common ingredients, in what I consider to be reasonable quantities, with optional items noted. The technique of searing and making the pan sauce remains the same.

THIS SAUCE ALSO GOES WELL WITH: any good steaks, venison, lamb chops, and veal scaloppini (refer to the tables on pages 208–26 for cooking tips).

YIELD: 2 SERVINGS

Two 4- to 5-ounce (115- to 140-g)
    beef tenderloin steaks, preferably
    no thicker than 1 inch/2.5 cm
Salt and freshly ground black pepper
3 tablespoons clarified butter
2 tablespoons minced shallots
    or scallion whites
1 clove garlic, minced (optional)
1/2 to 3/4 cup sliced or chopped
    mushrooms (omit if using truffles)
3 to 4 tablespoons Cognac or other
    brandy, Armagnac, or Madeira
1/2 cup good-quality, gelatin-rich beef
    stock, preferably homemade, or 1
    teaspoon demi-glace base, such
    as More than Gourmet brand,
    mixed with 1/2 cup warm water
1 teaspoon Dijon mustard (optional)
    > continues on next page

PREP

The steaks should be slightly cold; that will help prevent them from overcooking before the exterior is properly browned. Pat the steaks dry and season generously with salt and pepper.

SEAR

Heat a large skillet over medium-high to high heat. When it is hot, swirl in 2 tablespoons of the clarified butter. Arrange the steaks in the pan so they are evenly spaced. They should loudly sizzle as soon as they touch the hot surface. Sear until very brown on the first side, 2 to 3 minutes, then flip and cook to your desired temperature (see page 17). This may take only a minute or so more for rare; the second side may not be as well browned as the first. The internal temperature will increase slightly as the meat rests. Transfer the steaks to a clean platter or individual plates.

> continues on next page

1 to 2 teaspoons Worcestershire
   sauce (optional)
2 tablespoons heavy cream
   (optional)
2 tablespoons Madeira
About 2 tablespoons cold
   unsalted butter, cut into
   pats or small cubes
Freshly squeezed lemon
   juice (optional)
1 tablespoon snipped fresh chives
   or very finely chopped fresh
   parsley (omit if using truffles)
Shaved truffles (optional)

SAUCE

Let the pan cool for a minute. Discard the cooking fat and analyze the residue. A very dark brown, sticky fond is fine; if the fond
is black, crumbly, or flaky, wipe the pan clean before proceeding.
Return the skillet to medium heat, add the remaining tablespoon
of clarified butter, and sauté the shallots, optional garlic, and the
mushrooms, if using, until golden brown. Very carefully add the
Cognac and cook off most of the alcohol. Or, if you want to flambé
it (see page 137), have a pan lid handy to smother any flames that
make you uncomfortable. Tip the pan slightly away from you, to
protect your face, pour in the Cognac, and use a butane candle
lighter or long match to ignite the alcohol. Set the pan down on the
burner and let the alcohol burn off. Stir in the beef stock and simmer until the sauce is slightly syrupy and coats the back of a spoon.
Stir in the optional mustard, Worcestershire, and cream, and then
the Madeira, and bring back to a simmer. Stir in the cold butter one
piece at a time until just melted. Taste and adjust the seasoning with
salt, pepper, and/or a bit of lemon if desired.

Spoon the sauce over the steaks and sprinkle with the chives, or
shaved truffles, if you have them. Serve immediately.

TO FLAMBÉ OR NOT TO FLAMBÉ

There are few kitchen spectacles as captivating as the flambé. It is certainly a dramatic way to add liquor to a pan sauce, but it's not really necessary. Simmering the liquor does the same thing. Igniting liquid does not make it alcohol-free. Flambéing can potentially add a hint of flavor and burn off a bit of residual surface oil, but the changes are subtle at best. That doesn't mean you shouldn't do it. A safely executed flambé is exciting, so go ahead and give it a try. Just please be safe.

- Never be cavalier when you are working with high heat and alcohol. High-proof liquors do not need an open flame to ignite.
- Have a tight-fitting lid nearby. If you use a reasonable quantity of alcohol (no more than a few ounces), the flames will only last a few seconds before they burn out, but my rule is to extinguish anything that makes me nervous. Simply cover the pan with the lid so the flames are deprived of oxygen.
- Don't pour from the bottle. Measure out what you need into a separate container. Not only will this prevent the stream from catching on fire, it also avoids the possibility of overwhelming a sauce by overpouring.
- Be careful not to spill or drip the alcohol. Liquor on the pan handle, utensils, or stovetop can ignite.
- Don't wear loose sleeves and flouncy fabrics.
- Use a butane candle lighter or long matches.
- Protect your face and hands. Don't lean over a skillet when you add liquor. Tip the skillet away from you slightly and keep your head clear, or the flash could singe your face, eyebrows, and hair.

Rib Steaks with Whiskey "Béarnaise"

Béarnaise sauce is a derivative of a classic hollandaise made acidic with shallot-infused wine vinegar rather than lemon juice. It is commonly flavored with tarragon or tarragon vinegar, and the really good versions include a bit of concentrated meat glaze, or *glace de viande*. I've chosen to underplay the tarragon and put more emphasis on the meat glaze by building the sauce around the savory brown fond. Don't burn it! Consider "reverse searing," or cooking the steaks sous vide to a perfect medium-rare and then browning them in a hot skillet (see page 141). It works like a dream. (Cook down any collected juices from the cooking bag for an extra layer of fond.) Adding the whiskey helps to marry the rustic characteristics of a panfried rib steak with a fancy French sauce.

It can be tricky to make a good emulsified sauce, let alone one built with the additional steps of flambéing and deglazing. But if you want to test your pan-sauce prowess, this might be just the recipe for you. I highly recommend using an immersion blender, but if you don't have one, put the egg yolk in a heatproof bowl set over a saucepan of simmering water and very gradually whisk in the melted butter mixture.

THIS SAUCE ALSO GOES WELL WITH: salmon, halibut, and split lobster tails (refer to the tables on pages 208–26 for cooking tips).

**YIELD: 2 LARGE OR
4 MODERATE PORTIONS**

1 to 2 pounds (450 to 900 g) thick-cut rib steaks (1 inch/2.5 cm or more), bone-in or boneless
Salt and freshly ground black pepper
2 tablespoons clarified butter or neutral oil
2 tablespoons minced shallots
¼ cup tarragon vinegar
2 tablespoons whiskey
8 tablespoons (4 ounces/115 g/ 1 stick) unsalted butter, cut into pats or small cubes
1 egg yolk
1 to 2 tablespoons warm water, if needed

PREP

Heat the oven to 375°F/190°C.

Pat the steaks dry and season generously with salt and pepper.

SEAR

Heat a large ovenproof skillet over medium-high heat. When it is hot, swirl in just enough clarified butter to coat the bottom of the pan. Arrange the steaks in the pan so they are not touching. There should be a good, loud sizzle when the steaks touch the oil. Sear the steaks until browned on the first side, about 3 minutes.

Flip the steaks and put the pan in the oven. Cook the steaks, flipping them every 2 to 3 minutes, until they are just a few degrees below your desired temperature, about 7 minutes for medium-rare. (Chefs' recommended temperatures for medium-rare are 130° to 135°F/54° to 57°C.) The internal temperature will continue to increase a few degrees as the meat rests.

The pan handle will be very hot, so be sure to use an oven mitt from this point on. Transfer the steaks to a carving board to rest while you make the sauce.

SAUCE

Discard the cooking oil and cool the pan slightly. Analyze the pan residue. A very dark brown, sticky fond is fine; if the fond is black, crumbly, or flaky, wipe the pan clean before proceeding. Return the pan to medium heat and add the remaining clarified butter. Sauté the shallots until the raw crunch and aroma is cooked off, about 2 minutes.

To flambé the alcohol (see page 137), make sure you have a lid nearby to smother the flames if necessary. Very carefully add the whiskey, then tilt the pan away from you slightly and ignite the whiskey with a butane candle lighter or long match, being careful to protect your face and hands. The alcohol will burn off very quickly, but if any flames make you feel uncomfortable, smother them with the pan lid. When the flames have died down, deglaze the pan with the vinegar. Avoid breathing the fumes, or they may make you cough. Use a wooden spoon to dissolve any flavorful brown bits on the bottom of the pan, then reduce the vinegar by half. Add the butter and melt it completely. It's fine if it separates. Transfer the melted butter mixture to a measuring cup with a pouring spout; use a silicone spatula to make sure you get every drop.

Place the egg yolk in a tall, narrow container, ideally the cup that comes with an immersion blender. Place the blades of the immersion blender directly over the egg yolk and start to blend at medium-high speed. Gradually pour in the melted butter mixture, drawing up the blender as the sauce thickens and emulsifies.

> continues on next page

This should take only about 30 seconds. Or, if you don't have an immersion blender, put the egg yolk in a shallow metal bowl, set it over a saucepan of simmering water, and very gradually whisk the warm melted butter mixture into it. If the sauce is very thick, thin it with some or all of the warm water until it just runs from a spoon. Add ½ teaspoon salt, then taste and adjust the seasoning with additional salt, pepper, and/or vinegar if necessary.

Slice the steaks on the bias and arrange on individual plates or a clean platter. Spoon some of the sauce over the center of the slices and serve the remainder alongside.

PAN SAUCES AND SOUS-VIDE OR "REVERSE" COOKING METHODS

Searing is a fantastic way to finish steaks and other foods that have been cooked sous vide or at low temperatures. If you aren't familiar with those techniques, they are both methods for cooking at carefully controlled temperatures until foods reach the perfect "doneness," with little to no gradient between the exterior and interior. For instance, thick steaks can be sealed in a sous-vide bag and heated in 130°F/54°C water until they are a perfect medium-rare throughout. Cooking "in reverse" usually refers to steaks or roasts that are cooked to the preferred internal temperature in a low oven. The surface temperature never goes high enough for the foods to get brown or crispy on the outside, so for a crisp, brown exterior, they need to be finished with high heat, such as a quick sear in a hot skillet.

The searing process is basically the same as with raw meat or other ingredients. Thoroughly preheat the pan. Go ahead and nudge the temperature up a little hotter than usual, because you are only cooking the surface of the meat. Swirl in some oil, space the items evenly, and sear, turning as needed so the meat browns on all sides. Work quickly, or you may end up cooking the meat more than you wanted and defeating the whole purpose. After the meat is seared, proceed as you would with any fond. If you pour the collected meat juices from the sous-vide cooking bag into the skillet, they can be reduced into an extra layer of super-concentrated fond.

Buffalo or Beef Patties with Country Gravy

My father-in-law, a North Dakota railroad man, became a connoisseur of classic diner dishes during his time working the Northern Pacific Line. One dish that he has always loved but can't find much anymore is a good old-fashioned "hamburger steak": a ground beef patty seared nice and brown, served under a blanket of gravy. Country gravy is creamy and white. If you prefer brown gravy, see the Salisbury Steak variation below.

Ground buffalo or bison meat is more expensive than beef, but I think the flavor and lean, slightly crumbly texture is showcased better here than on a burger bun.

THIS SAUCE ALSO GOES WELL WITH: sausage patties, turkey patties, chicken, portobello mushroom caps, and skirt steak (refer to the tables on pages 208–26 for cooking tips).

YIELD: 4 SERVINGS

2 cups whole milk

Infusing ingredients (choose 2 or 3): a thin slice of onion or shallot, 4 or 5 black peppercorns, 1 bay leaf, 1 or 2 parsley stems, a carrot, and/or a garlic clove

1 pound (450 g) ground buffalo or lean ground beef, shaped into 4 thin oval patties

Salt and freshly ground black pepper

About 3 tablespoons neutral oil or unsalted butter

½ cup minced onion (optional)

3 tablespoons all-purpose flour

1 teaspoon Worcestershire sauce, or to taste

Dash of Tabasco sauce

PREP

Combine the milk and infusing ingredients in a medium saucepan or microwave-safe measuring cup and heat until the milk begins to steam and small bubbles form at the edges. Set the milk aside to infuse for 3 minutes, then strain, discarding the solids.

Season the patties generously with salt and pepper.

SEAR

Heat a large skillet over medium-high heat. When it is hot, swirl in just enough oil to coat the bottom. (If the meat is fatty, you may not need any cooking oil here.) Arrange the patties in the pan so they are evenly spaced: To properly fry, the patties must not be overcrowded. Each one should sizzle when it touches the hot pan. (If there is not enough room in the skillet to hold all the patties, cook them in batches.) Sear the patties until dark brown on the first side, about 3 minutes. Flip, reduce the heat slightly, and brown the other side. Then continue to cook, flipping the patties regularly, until cooked through (see page 17). Transfer the meat to a clean platter or individual plates and keep warm while you make the sauce.

SAUCE

This pan sauce is particularly reliant on the meaty flavor of a good pan residue. Unless the bits in the pan are clearly burnt, leave them. Do not discard the cooking fat. (Animal fats maintain their flavor with high heat better than vegetable fats.) Cool the pan slightly, then add more oil so there is a total of 3 tablespoons in the pan. Add the onions, if using, and sauté until soft, about 2 minutes. Remove the pan from the heat, sprinkle in the flour, and use a wooden spoon to stir the flour and fat into a paste (roux) and pick up any brown residue on the bottom of the pan. Return the pan to the burner and cook, stirring constantly, until the roux is bubbly and golden brown. Add half of the milk, stirring well to combine. Stir in the remainder of the milk and any juices that have collected under the meat patties. Season with a good pinch each of salt and pepper and simmer the gravy, stirring often, until it is thickened and coats the back of a spoon. Stir in the Worcestershire and Tabasco. Taste and adjust the seasoning as needed; the gravy should have a distinctive black pepper flavor.

Spoon enough gravy over the patties to moisten them and serve with the rest in a gravy boat alongside.

VARIATION:
SALISBURY STEAK WITH MUSHROOM SAUCE

It's easy to transform this recipe into another classic favorite, Salisbury steak, by smothering the patties in brown mushroom sauce instead of cream gravy.

Heat a tablespoon of oil or butter in the skillet after the patties have been browned. Sauté 1 cup sliced mushrooms with the minced onion until brown and tender, 2 to 3 minutes. Scoop the mushroom mixture from the skillet and set aside. Add 2 tablespoons oil or butter and continue the recipe as written, substituting beef stock for the infused milk. Stir the mushrooms into the finished gravy and season well before spooning it over the patties.

Pork Scaloppini with Bourbon-Molasses Glaze, Persimmons, and Pecans

Make sure you use flattish, firm Fuyu persimmons in this recipe. They are quite unlike the Hachiya variety, which is slightly bullet shaped and impossibly astringent until the fruit is meltingly soft. Fuyus are best enjoyed raw or gently warmed. Look for them in early autumn.

If you don't feel comfortable flambéing alcohol, just stir in the bourbon and let it simmer away.

THIS SAUCE ALSO GOES WELL WITH: turkey scaloppini, chicken cutlets, duck breasts, and sweet potato planks (refer to the tables on pages 208–26 for cooking tips).

**YIELD: 2 LARGE OR
4 MODERATE SERVINGS**

1 to 1½ pounds (450 to 675 g)
   boneless pork chops
   or pork loin slices
Salt and freshly ground black pepper
2 to 3 tablespoons all-purpose or
   rice flour for dredging (optional)
About 2 tablespoons clarified
   butter or neutral oil
2 tablespoons minced
   shallots or yellow onion
2 tablespoons bourbon
½ teaspoon ground ginger
¼ teaspoon cayenne
   pepper, or to taste
½ cup unfiltered apple
   cider or apple juice
2 tablespoons apple cider
   vinegar, or to taste
1 tablespoon brown sugar
1 tablespoon molasses

> *continues on next page*

PREP

Trim away any silver skin or membrane from the pork. If the chops are ½ inch thick or more, slice them in half by pressing on each one firmly with the palm of one hand, lifting your fingers out of the way, and then using long strokes of a sharp knife to slice it into 2 thinner cutlets.

Pound the pork into large, very thin scaloppini, no thicker than ¼ inch/0.6 cm. Pat dry and season generously with salt and pepper. Dredge the scaloppini in the flour, if using, and pat off the excess.

SEAR

Heat a large skillet over medium-high heat. Because the pork pieces are so large, they will need to be cooked in batches. When the pan is hot, add enough clarified butter to coat the bottom. Arrange 1 or 2 of the scaloppini in the pan, spacing them well apart. The pieces should sizzle the moment they touch the hot oil. Sear the scaloppini until browned on the first side, then flip and cook the other side; it will take only 3 to 4 minutes total until both sides are brown and the interior slightly pink. Transfer the pork to a clean platter and repeat with the remaining scaloppini.

1 to 2 tablespoons cold unsalted
   butter, cut into pats or small cubes

⅓ cup finely diced Fuyu persimmon

2 tablespoons chopped toasted
   pecans

SAUCE

Discard the cooking fat and analyze the pan residue. Remove any unappealing bits. Cool the pan slightly, then return it to medium heat. Swirl in a little fresh oil and sauté the shallots until just tender, about 1 minute.

If you want to flambé the alcohol (see page 137), have a lid nearby to smother the flames if necessary. Very carefully add the bourbon, then tilt the pan away from you slightly and ignite it with a butane candle lighter or long match, being careful to protect your face and hands. The alcohol will burn off very quickly, but if the flames make you feel at all uncomfortable, smother them with the pan lid. If you prefer not to flambé it, carefully pour the bourbon into the skillet, doing your best to keep the alcohol away from extreme heat or an open flame, and simmer until the liquid is reduced by about half.

Stir in the ginger and cayenne. Deglaze the pan with the apple cider, using a wooden spoon to dissolve any brown bits on the bottom of the pan. Add the vinegar, brown sugar, molasses and any juices that have collected under the pork, bring to a boil, and simmer until the liquid has reduced to a sticky, clinging syrup, about 2 minutes. Add a pinch of salt, then gradually stir in the butter, a few pieces at a time, until just melted. Taste and adjust the seasoning with salt, pepper, cayenne, and/or vinegar to taste.

Drizzle the sauce over the pork, sprinkle with the diced persimmons and toasted pecans, and serve.

Simmered Pork Chops with Carrot and Sriracha Reduction

While I was testing an idea for pork chops and carrot juice, I was interrupted by a friendly neighbor. When I returned to the skillet, the pork chops had become hard and rubbery. I begrudgingly wrote them off as a failure, but I decided to try and rescue our dinner by adding more carrot juice and simmering the chops until the tissues started to break down and they softened to succulence. It worked brilliantly. Once the chops were tender, I lifted them from the skillet and reduced the remaining liquid into an intense, concentrated sauce. The juices and rendered fat from the chops had infused their flavors into the sauce in the very best way, so I recommend that you choose bone-in chops with a fair amount of natural fat. If you are substituting another meat or other main ingredient, cook it until just done, then lift it onto a clean plate and cook down the sauce.

THIS SAUCE ALSO GOES WELL WITH: chicken pieces, cross-cut beef short ribs, split game hens, and tofu (refer to the tables on pages 208–26 for cooking tips).

YIELD: 2 LARGE OR 4 MODERATE SERVINGS

1½ to 2 pounds (675 to 900 g) bone-in pork chops (4)
Salt and freshly ground black pepper
About 1 tablespoon neutral oil
1 tablespoon minced fresh ginger
¾ cup carrot juice
½ cup low-sodium chicken stock, preferably homemade
1 tablespoon Sriracha sauce, or to taste
1 tablespoon unsalted butter (optional)
2 tablespoons minced fresh chives or thinly sliced scallions

PREP

Pat the pork chops dry and season generously with salt and pepper.

SEAR

Heat a large lidded sauté pan over medium-high heat. When it is hot, swirl in enough oil to coat the bottom. Arrange the pork chops in the pan so they are evenly spaced. They should sizzle the moment they touch the hot oil. (If there is not enough room in the pan for all of the pork, brown the meat in batches, wiping out the pan and adding fresh oil as needed.) Sear the chops until well browned on the first side, 3 to 4 minutes, then flip, reduce the temperature slightly, and brown the second side. The chops will not be cooked through at this point. Transfer them to a clean platter or plate.

SAUCE

Cool the pan slightly. Discard the cooking oil and analyze the pan residue. Remove any unappealing bits. Return the skillet to medium heat. Add a little fresh oil if the pan is very dry. Add the ginger and cook until aromatic and slightly softened, about 30 seconds. Deglaze the pan with the carrot juice, using a wooden spoon to dissolve any brown residue on the bottom of the skillet. Add the chicken stock and bring to a simmer, then return the chops and any collected juices to the pan. Cover the pan and simmer gently, flipping the chops occasionally, until tender, about 30 minutes. Lift the chops from the pan and transfer to a clean platter. Keep warm while you make the sauce.

Increase the temperature and reduce the cooking juices until they are the consistency of thin gravy. Stir in the Sriracha, taste, and adjust the seasoning with salt and pepper. Add the butter, if you like, for a bit of extra richness and gloss.

Spoon the sauce over the pork chops, sprinkle with the chives, and serve.

Pork Chops with Sour Cream and Sauerkraut Sauce,
served with steamed new potatoes

Pork Chops with Sour Cream and Sauerkraut Sauce

Slow-simmered pork and sauerkraut is one of my favorite cold-weather meals, so I wanted to come up with something that featured those flavors but was much quicker to cook. I originally imagined this as a very simple, creamy dish, but it got more savory and complex with every incarnation. I'm a big fan of live, fresh kraut, but the natural cultures are lost during the cooking process. Use fresh kraut if you make it or have a favorite brand. A good brown sear on the meat and a generous herb garnish help to liven up the color of this dish. I like to use classic bone-in pork rib chops, sliced neither thick nor thin. The bones and additional bit of fat make them more flavorful than boneless loin cuts.

THIS SAUCE ALSO GOES WELL WITH: smoked sausages, calf's liver, cod, meatballs, and chicken pieces (refer to the tables on pages 208–26 for cooking tips).

YIELD: 4 SERVINGS

1 teaspoon kosher salt,
    plus more to taste
1 teaspoon juniper berries
½ teaspoon caraway seeds
¼ teaspoon cayenne pepper
2 to 2½ pounds (900 g to 1 kg)
    bone-in pork rib chops (4)
Freshly ground black pepper
2 to 3 tablespoons all-purpose
    flour for dredging (optional)
About 2 tablespoons neutral
    oil or clarified butter
⅓ cup minced yellow onion
2 cloves garlic, minced
½ cup Riesling or similar
    off-dry white wine
1 cup low-sodium chicken stock,
    preferably homemade
2 fresh bay leaves or 1 dried bay leaf

> *continues on next page*

PREP

Combine the salt, juniper berries, caraway seeds, and cayenne pepper in a spice or coffee mill and grind to a fine powder. Set aside.

Pat the pork dry and season with salt and pepper. Dredge the chops with the flour, if using, and pat off the excess.

SEAR

Heat a large skillet over medium-high heat. When it is hot, swirl in enough oil to thinly coat the bottom. Arrange the pork chops in the pan so they are evenly spaced. They should sizzle the moment they touch the hot oil. (If there is not enough room in the pan for all of the meat, cook the pork in batches, wiping the pan clean and starting with fresh oil as needed.) Sear the chops until well browned on the first side, 3 to 4 minutes, then flip, reduce the temperature slightly, and brown the second side. The chops will not be cooked through at this point. Transfer them to a clean platter or plate.

> *continues on next page*

1½ teaspoons freshly
ground black pepper

½ cup sour cream

1 cup coarsely chopped sauerkraut,
rinsed if you prefer a milder flavor

Chopped fresh herbs, such as
parsley, chives, or dill, for garnish

SAUCE

Discard the cooking oil and analyze the pan residue. Remove any unappealing bits or scorched flour. Cool the pan slightly, then return it to medium heat; if it is very dry, add a little fresh oil. Sauté the onions until soft and lightly browned, about 3 minutes. Add the garlic and cook until the aroma blooms, about 20 seconds. Stir in the ground spice mixture. Deglaze the pan with the wine, using a wooden spoon to dissolve any residue on the bottom of the skillet. Increase the temperature and simmer until the aroma of raw alcohol is gone and the volume has reduced by half.

Add the chicken stock and bay leaves to the pan. Return the pork chops and any collected liquid to the pan and simmer, flipping the pork chops often, until just cooked through and tender, about 4 minutes for ¾-inch/2-cm-thick chops. For the best flavor and texture, they should remain just barely pink inside.

Lift the chops onto a clean platter or individual plates. Boil the sauce until it thickens to the consistency of gravy. Fish out and discard the bay leaves. Stir in the sauerkraut.

The sour cream needs to be added carefully, or it will break into tiny beads. First temper it by putting it into a small bowl and stirring in 2 or 3 spoonfuls of the warm sauce, until the sour cream is warm and pourable, then stir the mixture into the sauce; do not boil once the sour cream has been added. Add the black pepper, then taste and adjust the seasoning with salt and a pinch more cayenne if desired.

Spoon the sauce over the chops, garnish with the chopped herbs, and serve.

Lamb Chops with Pomegranate Reduction and Spiced Yogurt Drizzle

There is nothing complicated about this recipe—the trickiest bit is getting the lamb chops cooked just right—but it seems fancy and elaborate. It's a great dinner party dish because the lamb chops, pomegranate reduction, and yogurt drizzle all hold quite well. Keep them separate until you are ready for the main course, then reheat each element as needed, assemble the dish, garnish, and serve.

The instructions here are for loin chops, which look like miniature T-bone steaks. If you prefer to serve rack of lamb, sear the rack whole and then pan-roast it to your desired temperature before slicing into individual chops.

THIS SAUCE ALSO GOES WELL WITH: skin-on "airline" chicken breasts, mackerel fillets, semi-boneless quail, duck breasts, and eggplant (refer to the tables on pages 208–26 for cooking tips).

YIELD: 4 SERVINGS

2 to 2½ pounds (900 to 1 kg) lamb loin chops (8)

2 tablespoons olive or neutral oil

2 cups unsweetened pomegranate juice

½ cup plain yogurt or goat's-milk yogurt

½ teaspoon ground cinnamon

½ teaspoon ground cumin

½ teaspoon ground ginger

½ teaspoon kosher salt

Pinch of cayenne pepper

1 tablespoon water, or as needed

⅓ cup chopped lightly salted roasted pistachios

1 tablespoon chopped fresh mint

Pomegranate seeds for garnish (optional)

PREP

Pat the chops dry and season generously with salt and pepper.

SEAR

Heat a large skillet over medium-high heat. When the pan is hot, swirl in just enough oil to coat the bottom. Arrange the chops in the pan so they are evenly spaced. They should sizzle the moment they hit the oil. Brown the chops on one side, about 3 minutes, then flip and reduce the temperature slightly. Loin chops can be almost block-shaped, so the sides may also need browning. Continue to cook, adjusting the temperature and flipping the meat as needed, until the chops are just a degree or two below your preferred temperature (see page 17). The internal temperature will increase a bit as the meat rests. If while you are browning the lamb, the pan residue seems to be getting very dark before the chops are done, remove them and deglaze the pan with some of the pomegranate juice. Save the deglazing liquid, wipe the pan clean, and continue searing the chops with fresh oil. Transfer the chops to a clean platter or plate and keep warm while you make the sauce.

> *continues on next page*

SAUCE

Cool the skillet slightly, then discard the cooking oil and analyze the residue. A very dark brown, sticky fond is fine; if the fond is black, crumbly, or flaky, wipe the pan clean before proceeding. Deglaze the skillet with the pomegranate juice. Use a wooden spoon to dissolve any flavorful brown residue on the bottom of the pan, then add any deglazing liquid you collected when searing the chops. Bring the juice to a boil, skim the surface to remove any scum or unappealing bits, and continue to boil until the juice is the consistency of warm honey. (The final volume will be only a few tablespoons.)

While the juice is boiling, make the yogurt drizzle: Stir together the yogurt, cinnamon, cumin, ginger, salt, and cayenne in a bowl. Add enough water to make the yogurt fluid enough to drizzle from a spoon.

To serve, drizzle the warm pomegranate reduction over the lamb chops, followed by the spiced yogurt, and then sprinkle with the chopped pistachios, mint, and pomegranate seeds, if using.

Lamb Chops with Pomegranate Reduction and
Spiced Yogurt Drizzle (page 151)

Lamb Steaks with
Simple, Fresh-Tasting Tomato Sauce

This tomato sauce from *Mastering Sauces* is one of my favorites—so much so that I had to include it here too. It's incredibly quick and adaptable. It can be enhanced with chiles, various spices, minced ham or bacon, and almost any herbs. I simmer it for a very short time in order to maintain the fresh tomato flavor and texture, rather than develop the thicker, sweeter characteristics of slow-cooked sauces. Of course, the better the canned tomatoes, the better the sauce.

Lamb steaks aren't as tender as chops, but I don't mind because the low price and good flavor make them a more suitable weeknight meal. Choose steaks cut from the leg, not the shoulder.

THIS SAUCE ALSO GOES WELL WITH: chicken, meatballs or patties, Italian or vegetarian sausages, eggplant, and polenta cakes (refer to the tables on pages 208–26 for cooking tips).

**YIELD: 2 LARGE OR
4 MODERATE SERVINGS**

1 to 1½ pounds (450 to 675 g)
   lamb leg steaks (2 large)
Salt and freshly ground black pepper
2 tablespoons olive or neutral oil
½ cup diced yellow onion
2 to 3 cloves garlic, chopped
¼ teaspoon red chile
   flakes, or to taste
½ cup dry white wine, such as
   Pinot Gris, or dry vermouth
One 14.5-ounce (411-g) diced
   tomatoes in juice, or whole
   tomatoes, crushed, juices reserved
2 teaspoons chopped fresh rosemary

PREP

Pat the steaks dry with paper towels. Season generously with salt and pepper.

SEAR

Heat a large lidded sauté pan over medium-high heat. When it is hot, swirl in just enough oil to coat the bottom. Arrange the steaks in the pan so they are evenly spaced. They should sizzle the moment they touch the hot oil. Sear the steaks until dark brown on the first side, about 3 minutes. Flip, reduce the heat slightly, and brown the second side. Then continue to cook, flipping regularly, until the steaks reach your preferred internal temperature, about 5 to 6 minutes for medium (see page 17). The temperature will increase slightly as the meat rests. Lift the steaks onto a clean platter or plate and keep warm while you make the sauce.

SAUCE

Cool the skillet slightly. Discard the cooking oil and analyze the pan residue. Remove any unappealing bits. A very dark brown, sticky fond is fine; if the residue is black, crumbly, or flaky, wipe the pan clean before proceeding. Return the pan to medium-heat and add the remaining oil. Sauté the onions until soft, about 3 minutes. Stir in the garlic and chiles and cook until the aroma of the garlic blooms, about 20 seconds. Deglaze the pan with the wine, using a wooden spoon to dissolve any brown residue on the bottom of the skillet. Simmer until the raw aroma of the alcohol is gone and the volume has reduced by half.

Stir in the tomatoes, with their juices, the rosemary, any juices that have collected on the plate with the lamb, and a pinch each of salt and pepper. Simmer until the sauce has thickened enough to be cohesive while remaining quite fluid, loose, and fresh tasting, no more than 3 or 4 minutes. Taste and adjust the seasoning with salt and pepper.

Return the steaks to the pan, flip to coat in the sauce, and gently reheat, about another minute. (If you prefer your lamb braised until quite tender, you can cover the pan and simmer everything together until the steaks are very tender, about 25 minutes more, adding a bit of water if the sauce becomes too thick. The flavor and texture of the sauce will be changed.)

Lift the steaks onto a clean platter or individual plates. Spoon enough sauce over the meat to moisten it and serve the rest alongside.

Lamb Patties with Berbere Gravy and Fresh Cheese Topping

Berbere, a flaming-hot spice mix popular in Ethiopia and Eritrea, has been gaining attention lately. Jars of "berbere seasoning" are now available at my local supermarket, but I love exploring specialty grocers, and the bags I've found at African markets are much spicier. Another ingredient popular in some African kitchens is Jumbo or Maggi brand seasoning cubes. They are essentially umami bombs dressed up as soft bouillon cubes. As a more accessible, MSG-free alternative, I have substituted soy sauce, but if you have Maggi or Jugo liquid seasonings or Bragg's liquid amino acids on hand, use them instead.

"Fresh cheese" describes milk curds that have been drained of whey but have not been fully dried or aged. Variations can be found in nearly every dairy-loving country. I have used drained cottage cheese, dollops of low-fat ricotta, or even thick Greek yogurt. Any of them is a cool and welcome contrast to the spicy sauce.

THIS SAUCE ALSO GOES WELL WITH: beef, turkey, or chicken patties (as written); lamb chops; whole fish; and salmon (refer to the tables on pages 208–26 for cooking tips).

YIELD: 4 SERVINGS

1 pound (450 g) ground lamb

¼ cup whole milk

3 tablespoons unseasoned bread crumbs

1 large egg, beaten

1 teaspoon kosher salt, or to taste

2 tablespoons neutral oil

½ cup minced onion

½ cup minced red bell pepper

½ cup minced tomato

1 tablespoon berbere (see headnote)

1 tablespoon all-purpose flour

1 cup low-sodium beef or chicken stock, preferably homemade

1 tablespoon soy sauce, Maggi or Jugo seasoning, or Bragg's liquid amino acids, or to taste

> *continues on next page*

PREP

Combine the ground lamb, milk, egg, bread crumbs, and salt in a bowl and mix with your hands until cohesive and smooth. Shape the lamb into 8 even patties about ½ inch/1.25 cm thick. I make them oval rather than round, because these seem to fit better in the skillet.

SEAR

Heat a large skillet over medium-high heat. When the pan is hot, swirl in just enough oil to coat the bottom. Arrange the lamb patties in the pan so they are evenly spaced. They should sizzle the moment they touch the hot oil. (Do not overcrowd the pan. If necessary, cook the lamb in batches, wiping out the pan and starting with fresh oil.) Brown the patties thoroughly on the first side, 2 to 3 minutes. Flip, reduce the heat slightly, and brown the second side. Then continue to cook, flipping regularly, until the patties are just cooked through, about 3 to 4 minutes longer. The internal

Freshly ground black pepper

⅓ cup fresh cheese, such as cottage cheese, farm cheese, or ricotta

2 tablespoons sliced scallion greens

temperature will continue to rise as the meat rests. (The patties will be reheated in the sauce, so don't worry if they are slightly pink inside at this point.) Lift the patties onto a clean platter or plate and keep warm while you make the sauce.

SAUCE

Cool the skillet slightly. Discard the cooking oil and analyze the residue. Remove any unappealing bits. A very dark brown, sticky fond is fine; if the fond is black, crumbly, or flaky, wipe the pan clean before proceeding. Return the skillet to medium-high heat. Add the remaining oil and sauté the onions and peppers until the onions are golden brown and just tender, about 3 minutes. Stir in the garlic and ginger and cook until the aroma blooms, about 20 seconds.

Remove the skillet from the burner, sprinkle in the flour, and use a wooden spoon to stir and pick up any flavorful residue on the bottom of the pan. (Removing the pan from the heat allows you to mix the roux without rushing and helps prevent lumps.) Return the pan to the heat and cook, stirring, until the roux bubbles and browns slightly. Stir in the tomatoes, using the wooden spoon to mix in any flour and remaining brown residue on the bottom of the pan. Add the berbere, stir in the stock and soy sauce, and bring to a simmer.

Return the patties to the pan, flip to coat with the sauce, and simmer until the sauce has reduced to the consistency of gravy, 3 to 4 minutes. Taste and adjust the seasoning with salt, pepper, and/or soy sauce if necessary.

Lift the patties onto a serving platter or individual plates. Spoon over the sauce and top with small dollops of the cheese. Sprinkle with the sliced scallion greens and serve.

Italian Sausages with Bell Pepper Relish

It doesn't take much to make great Italian sausages, peppers, and onions, so I've done my best to keep this recipe simple. Finely chopping the vegetables and then cooking them until they are soft really sweetens them up. A few seasonings and a drizzle of good olive oil is all that it takes to pull them into a warm, saucy relish.

If you can find them, use late-summer Italian "frying peppers," or cubanelles. This is one of the only recipes in the book where I use extra-virgin olive oil for frying. It is the best choice here.

THIS SAUCE ALSO GOES WELL WITH: chicken, halibut, lamb, eggplant, and provolone "steaks" (refer to the tables on pages 208–26 for cooking tips).

YIELD: 4 SERVINGS

1 to 1½ pounds (450 to 675 g) hot or mild fresh Italian sausages (4 to 6 links)

1 tablespoon olive oil or neutral oil, or as needed

½ cup water

2 cups finely chopped sweet "frying peppers" (also called cubanelles) or red, yellow, and/or green bell peppers

About ¼ cup extra-virgin olive oil

½ cup finely chopped sweet onion, such as Walla Walla Sweet

4 cloves garlic, chopped

Pinch of red chile flakes (optional)

½ teaspoon kosher salt

Freshly ground black pepper

1 teaspoon dried oregano

¼ cup dry white wine, such as Sauvignon Blanc or Pinot Gris, or extra-dry vermouth

1 tablespoon red wine vinegar

PREP

Prick the sausages a few times to prevent them from bursting. There are some cooks who don't recommend this because pricking lets the juices run out rather than remaining in the casings, but here the juices are incorporated into the sauce. Pat the sausages dry with paper towels.

SEAR

Heat a large covered sauté pan over medium heat. When it is hot, swirl in just enough neutral oil to coat the bottom of the pan. Arrange the sausages in the pan and slowly and evenly brown them on all sides, about 4 minutes. Add the water, being careful to avoid the steam that will immediately form, and cover the pan. Reduce the heat and simmer the sausages for 6 to 7 minutes, until they are cooked through (160°F/70°C). Lift the sausages out of the pan onto a clean plate and keep warm while you make the sauce.

SAUCE

Simmer any juices remaining in the pan until they are reduced to a sticky brown residue. Add about a tablespoon of the olive oil and sauté the peppers and onions until they are softened and the pan is quite dry, 3 to 4 minutes. Stir in the garlic, chile flakes, if using, salt, pepper, and oregano and cook for another minute. Deglaze the pan with the wine and vinegar. Drizzle in enough of the remaining olive oil to bring everything together into a loose relish. Taste and adjust the seasoning as needed, then return the sausages to the pan to warm through.

Lift the sausages onto a platter or individual plates, spoon the sauce over them, and serve.

Kielbasa with Ketchup and Curry Sauce, served with green salad.

Kielbasa with Ketchup and Curry Sauce

I wish I could come up with a clever name to make this dish sound as fantastic as it tastes. I've served it to several skeptical diners and never once had leftovers. The kielbasa is split and then browned until dark and crispy at the edges. The beer-laced pan sauce is thick with sautéed onions, spices, and the pleasing, familiar tang of ketchup. Fully cooked smoked German sausages or cooked bratwurst can be substituted for the kielbasa if you prefer.

THIS SAUCE ALSO GOES WELL WITH: ground beef or buffalo patties, ham steaks, fish cakes, and chicken legs (refer to the tables on pages 208–26 for cooking tips).

YIELD: 3 OR 4 SERVINGS

One 14- to 16-ounce (400-
   to 450-g) kielbasa
1 tablespoon neutral oil
1 cup sliced yellow onion
1 tablespoon mild or hot
   curry powder
½ cup beer, such as lager or pilsner
   (nonalcoholic beer is fine)
⅓ cup ketchup
Freshly ground black pepper
1 tablespoon unsalted
   butter (optional)

PREP

Cut the kielbasa into 4 equal segments. Split the segments lengthwise so you have 8 pieces.

SEAR

Heat a large skillet over medium heat. When the pan is hot, swirl in just enough oil to coat the bottom. Arrange the sausage pieces evenly in the pan, cut side down, and sear until dark brown and crispy, about 3 minutes. Transfer to a clean platter or plate.

SAUCE

Discard the cooking oil and analyze the pan residue. Remove any unappealing bits or burnt residue. Cool the pan slightly, then return it to medium heat. Swirl in any remaining oil and sauté the onions until browned and tender, 3 to 4 minutes. Stir in the curry powder. Deglaze the pan with the beer, using a wooden spoon to dissolve any brown residue on the bottom of the skillet. The beer will be very foamy at first but will subside. Simmer until the raw scent of alcohol is gone. Add the ketchup, return the kielbasa to the pan, and cook, flipping occasionally, until fully heated through, 2 to 3 minutes.

Add the butter and stir until it just melts into the sauce. Taste and adjust the seasoning with salt as needed and plenty of black pepper. Lift the kielbasa onto a clean platter or individual plates, spoon the sauce over, and serve.

Bangers with Onion and Brown Ale Gravy

Bangers are mild English or Irish sausages. I absolutely adore them, especially when they are smothered with an onion and ale gravy. It's been a rainy-day favorite of ours for decades. This recipe makes a *lot* of gravy, because I always serve it with a heap of mashed potatoes. I'd originally planned to scale back the amount, but that idea was kiboshed by tasters who slurped up every last drop.

THIS SAUCE ALSO GOES WELL WITH: skirt steak, pork chops, chicken thighs, and meatballs or patties, (refer to the tables on pages 208–26 for cooking tips).

YIELD: 4 TO 6 SERVINGS

4 to 6 English or Irish "bangers" (mild pork sausages; about 4 ounces/115 g each)
About 1 teaspoon neutral oil
½ cup water
2 tablespoons unsalted butter
1 medium sweet onion, such as Walla Walla Sweet, sliced (about 2 cups)
1 tablespoon all-purpose flour
½ cup English ale, such as Newcastle Brown Ale (or substitute another slightly malty rather than bitter ale)
1 cup low-sodium beef or chicken stock, preferably homemade
1 tablespoon Worcestershire sauce
Salt and freshly ground black pepper
2 tablespoons chopped fresh parsley (optional)

PREP

Prick the sausages in a few places to prevent them from bursting as they cook. There are some cooks who don't recommend this because it lets the juices run out rather than stay in the casings, but they are called "bangers" for good reason—and any juices that escape will eventually be incorporated into the pan sauce. Pat the sausages dry with paper towels.

SEAR

Heat a large lidded sauté pan over medium heat. When it is hot, swirl in just enough oil to coat the bottom. Add the sausages and brown them evenly on all sides, about 4 minutes.

Pour in the water, cover the pan, reduce the heat slightly, and gently simmer until the sausages are fully cooked through, 5 to 7 minutes, depending on how large they are. (The USDA recommends that sausages be cooked to an internal temperature of 160°F/71°C.) Lift the bangers out of the pan onto a clean platter or plate and keep warm while you make the sauce.

SAUCE

If there is any liquid left in the pan, reduce it to a sticky brown residue. Add the butter, and when it is melted and foamy, stir in the onions. Cook, stirring often, until brown and soft, about 6 minutes.

Remove the pan from the heat, sprinkle in the flour, and stir to mix. (Removing the pan from the heat allows you to mix the roux without rushing, which reduces the risk of lumps.) Return the pan to the heat and cook, stirring constantly, until the flour is golden brown, about 1 minute. Deglaze the pan with the ale. Use a wooden spoon to loosen and dissolve the browned roux and residue on the bottom of the pan. Simmer until the aroma of raw alcohol has cooked off. Stir in the stock, return the sausages to the pan, and simmer, uncovered, until the gravy has thickened and the flavor has concentrated, about 5 minutes. Stir in the Worcestershire sauce. Taste and adjust the seasoning with salt and pepper if desired.

Lift the bangers onto a clean platter or individual plates and spoon some of the gravy over the top. Sprinkle with the parsley and serve with the rest of the gravy alongside.

Ham Steak with Red Currant and Garam Masala Syrup

I always feel terribly clever when I spot ham steaks at the market and remember how quickly they can become a simple, satisfying meal. I tend to forget about them, even though we have some very good local producers. Since ham steaks are already cooked, all it takes is a quick sear to bring out the flavor. This sauce is essentially three ingredients: red currant jelly, garam masala, and butter. If you want to make it "fancier," stir in a little fresh lime juice and a few fresh or frozen red currants. Frozen red currants can be found in Scandinavian, Russian, and some specialty markets.

Garam masala, a blend of "warming" spices, is a popular seasoning for various Indian dishes. The predominant flavors include cloves, cinnamon, and ginger, all of which go well with ham. Black pepper, cardamom, coriander, and cumin make it more complex.

THIS SAUCE ALSO GOES WELL WITH: duck breasts, lamb chops, turkey or pork scaloppini, and sweet potato planks (refer to the tables on pages 208–26 for cooking tips).

YIELD: 2 LARGE OR 4 MODERATE SERVINGS

1 cooked ham steak (about 1 to 1½ pounds/450 to 675 g)
3 tablespoons red currant jelly
½ teaspoon garam masala
About 2 teaspoons neutral oil
1 tablespoon unsalted butter
Salt and freshly ground black pepper
1 tablespoon freshly squeezed lemon or lime juice (optional)
2 tablespoons fresh or frozen red currants (optional)

PREP

Pat the ham dry. Stir together the jelly and garam masala in a small bowl.

SEAR

Heat a large skillet over medium to medium-high heat. Swirl in just enough oil to coat the bottom of the pan. Sear the ham, turning once, until it is browned on both sides and heated through, about 3 minutes on each side. Lift the ham onto a clean platter.

SAUCE

Cool the skillet slightly, then deglaze the pan with the jelly mixture, using a wooden spoon to dissolve any brown residue on the bottom of the pan. Add the butter and stir until it is just melted. Taste and adjust the seasoning with salt and pepper if needed. Add the lime juice and currants, if using. Spoon the sauce over the ham steak and serve.

Veal Scaloppini with Leek and Tomato Beurre Blanc

Beurre blanc is a traditional white wine butter sauce. Let me put a particularly heavy emphasis on the word *butter* here. The volume of the sauce is higher than in my other recipes, but that's because I have yet to find a better way to serve veal scaloppini than with a quick sear and a buttery sauce. The veal should be golden brown but still pink in the middle. To prevent the meat from overcooking, focus on browning the first side well, then flip and lightly cook the other side for a perfect interior temperature.

THIS SAUCE ALSO GOES WELL WITH: sole, chicken or turkey scaloppini, cod, and salmon (refer to the tables on pages 208–26 for cooking tips).

YIELD: 3 OR 4 SERVINGS

1 pound (450 g) veal scaloppini

Salt and finely ground white pepper

2 to 3 tablespoons all-purpose flour for dredging

2 tablespoons clarified butter or neutral oil

⅓ cup thinly sliced leeks (white and very pale green parts only)

2 tablespoons white balsamic or tarragon vinegar

⅓ cup extra-dry vermouth

⅓ cup finely diced tomato (preferably skinned and seeded)

4 tablespoons (2 ounces/60 g/ ½ stick) cold unsalted butter, cut into cut into pats or small cubes

PREP

Pat the veal dry and season with salt and white pepper. Dredge in the flour and pat off the excess.

SEAR

Heat a large skillet over medium-high heat. When it is hot, add just enough clarified butter to evenly coat the bottom. Arrange the veal in the pan so the pieces are evenly spaced. They should sizzle the moment they touch the hot oil. (If there is not enough room in the pan for all of the pieces, cook the veal in batches, wiping the pan clean and starting with fresh butter as needed.) Sear the scaloppini until well browned on the first side, about 4 minutes, then flip, reduce the temperature slightly, and cook until lightly browned on the second side but still slightly pink inside. The internal temperature will increase slightly as the meat rests. Transfer the veal to a clean platter or plate and keep warm while you make the sauce.

> continues on next page

SAUCE

Cool the skillet slightly. Discard the fat and analyze the pan residue. Remove any unappealing bits or scorched flour. Return the pan to medium heat and add the remaining clarified butter. Sauté the leeks until wilted but not browned, about 30 seconds. Deglaze the pan with the vinegar, being careful to avoid the fumes, or they may make you cough. Use a wooden spoon to dissolve any residue on the bottom of the pan. When the vinegar has mostly evaporated, add the vermouth and simmer until the aroma of raw alcohol is gone and the volume has reduced by half. Stir in the tomatoes. Gradually stir the butter, a few pieces at a time, until just melted; do not boil the sauce after the butter has been added. Taste and adjust the seasoning with salt and white pepper, then return the veal and any collected juices to the pan, flip to coat with sauce, and warm gently.

Lift the scaloppini onto a clean platter or individual plates and spoon the sauce over. Serve immediately.

Ingredients for Leek and
Tomato Beurre Blanc (page
165): vermouth, butter, leeks,
tomatoes

Seared Calf's Liver with Warm Salsa Criolla

The fact that you are reading this means you are a liver lover or know one. And you probably already know how well fried liver goes with pan sauces. If not, you are in for a treat! Calf's liver is much harder to find than beef liver, but it is far milder and worth seeking out. You may need to find a specialty butcher or even buy it frozen. Beef liver can be substituted, but I suggest soaking it in a milk or water bath for at least an hour to help mellow the flavor slightly. Dry it well before dredging.

Salsa criolla is similar to pico de gallo, but it's not spicy. It also has a much brighter flavor because of the vinegar. It's not traditionally served hot, but I like it better with the onions softened slightly over heat.

THIS SAUCE ALSO GOES WELL WITH: steaks, sea bass, rockfish, chicken, and provolone "steaks" (refer to the tables on pages 208–26 for cooking tips).

YIELD: 4 SERVINGS

1 pound (450 g) calf's liver, cleaned
    and sliced (see headnote)
Salt and freshly ground black pepper
¼ cup all-purpose flour for dredging
½ cup neutral or olive oil
½ cup minced onion
2 cloves garlic, minced
Pinch of red chile flakes (optional)
3 tablespoons red wine
    vinegar, or to taste
½ cup minced tomato
¼ cup minced red or
    green bell pepper
½ teaspoon dried oregano
2 tablespoons chopped fresh
    parsley (optional)

PREP

Pat the liver slices dry and season generously with salt and pepper. Dredge in the flour and pat off the excess.

SEAR

Heat a large sauté pan over medium-high to high heat. When it is hot, swirl in enough oil to coat the bottom. Arrange the liver slices so they are evenly spaced. They should sizzle the moment they touch the hot oil. (If there is not enough room in the pan for all of the meat, cook it in batches, cleaning the pan and starting with fresh oil as needed.) Sear the liver until the first side is nice and browned, about 2 to 3 minutes, then flip, reduce the heat slightly, and cook until it is just pink in the center, another minute or two. (Or continue to flip the meat and cook it to your preference.) Transfer the liver to a clean platter and keep warm while you make the sauce.

SAUCE

Cool the skillet slightly. Discard the frying oil and wipe out any burnt residue or scorched flour. Return the pan to medium heat and swirl in the remaining oil. Sauté the onions until aromatic and barely softened, about 1 minute. Add the garlic and chile flakes, if using, and stir to mix. Pour in the vinegar, being careful to avoid breathing the fumes, or they may make you cough. Use a wooden spoon to dissolve any brown residue on the bottom of the pan. Stir in the tomato, bell pepper, oregano, and parsley, if using. Season generously with salt and pepper. The sauce should be quite salty and bright, so add a bit more vinegar if needed and stir until just warmed through.

Spoon the sauce over the liver and serve.

VEGETABLES AND EGGS

Crispy Tofu with Peanut and Red Curry Pan Sauce

I do my best to respect culinary traditions and make authentic preparations whenever I can, which inevitably means I have a ton of diverse ingredients on hand. Now and then I'll improvise and mash up whatever complementary ingredients are within easy reach. That's how this pan sauce came to be. Sometimes I use a splash of stock instead of the coconut milk, or add some minced lemongrass or Indonesian shrimp paste. I'm including this recipe as a reminder that you can create an original pan sauce without relying on classic French ingredients or techniques.

THIS SAUCE ALSO GOES WELL WITH: shrimp, chicken, pork, broccoli, paneer, eggplant, and sweet potato planks (refer to the tables on pages 208–26 for cooking tips).

YIELD: 2 OR 3 SERVINGS

One 1-pound (450-g) block firm tofu, drained

2 to 3 tablespoons rice flour for dredging

About 2 tablespoons peanut or neutral oil

2 cloves garlic, chopped

1 tablespoon minced fresh ginger

2 teaspoons Thai red curry paste (or substitute Penang curry paste)

1 cup coconut milk

3 tablespoons unsweetened natural peanut butter (smooth or chunky)

2 teaspoons brown sugar or grated palm sugar, or to taste

2 tablespoons freshly squeezed lime juice, or to taste

1 tablespoon fish sauce (substitute soy sauce for a vegan or vegetarian dish), or to taste

Salt

2 tablespoons thinly sliced scallion greens

PREP

This step is optional, but I think it improves the flavor and texture: To freshen the tofu, put it in a bowl, pour over boiling water to cover, and let sit for 5 minutes. Drain and pat dry with paper towels. To press out excess water you can put the block of tofu between two plates and weight the top one with a soup can for 10 minutes.

Cut the tofu into 6 to 8 slices. Dredge the pieces in the rice flour, patting off the excess.

SEAR

Heat a large skillet over medium-high heat. When it is hot, swirl in enough oil to generously coat the bottom. Arrange the tofu in the pan so the pieces are evenly spaced. They should sizzle the moment they touch the hot oil. (If there is not enough room for all of the tofu, cook it in batches, adding more oil as needed.) Sear the tofu until it is golden brown and crisp on the first side, 2 to 3 minutes, then flip, reduce the heat slightly, and brown the second side. Transfer the tofu to clean platter or individual plates. Or, if you want the tofu to remain crisp on all sides, put it on a baking rack and keep it in a warm oven while you make the sauce, then plate it.

SAUCE

Discard the frying oil and remove any unappealing bits. (Unlike meat or seafood, tofu doesn't leave a flavorful fond.) Cool the pan slightly, then return the skillet to medium heat and add a small amount of oil. Sauté the garlic and ginger until the aroma has bloomed but they have not browned, about 20 seconds. Stir in the curry paste, then gradually add the coconut milk, stirring constantly until blended. Add the peanut butter and sugar and bring the sauce to a simmer. Cook for 2 to 3 minutes, stirring constantly, until the sauce is thickened and the flavors have infused. Add the lime juice and fish sauce, taste, and adjust the seasoning with salt, sugar, fish sauce, and/or lime juice as you like.

Spoon enough sauce over the tofu to evenly moisten it and sprinkle with the scallion greens. Serve with the remaining sauce alongside.

Crispy Tofu with 3-Ingredient Teriyaki Sauce, served over rice with kimchee and additional sauce alongside

Crispy Tofu with 3-Ingredient Teriyaki Sauce

Why would anyone buy bottled teriyaki sauce when you can whip up a fresh batch with only three ingredients? I make it all the time using a ratio I learned from an old line cook: 4 parts soy sauce, 2 parts sugar, and 1 part mirin. A Japanese rice wine, a super-sweet brand of mirin, is available in the specialty foods section of many supermarkets; if you have a source for authentic Japanese ingredients, consider buying something a little better to add more fermented, slightly yeasty nuances. If you prefer a more complex teriyaki sauce, embellish this with some minced garlic or ginger, sesame seeds, chile sauce, or a full teaspoon of ground black pepper as it simmers.

THIS SAUCE ALSO GOES WELL WITH: salmon, snapper, steak, chicken, pork, broccoli, and eggplant (refer to the tables on pages 208–26 for cooking tips).

YIELD: 2 OR 3 SERVINGS

One 1-pound (450-g) block
   firm tofu, drained
2 to 3 tablespoons rice
   flour for dredging
About 2 tablespoons
   peanut or neutral oil
½ cup soy sauce
¼ cup sugar
2 tablespoons mirin
2 tablespoons thinly sliced
   scallion greens

PREP

This step is optional, but I think the flavor and texture are improved: To freshen the tofu, put it in a bowl, pour over boiling water to cover, and let sit for 5 minutes. Drain and pat dry with paper towels. To press out additional water, you can put the block of tofu between two plates and weight the top one with a soup can for 10 minutes.

Cut the tofu into 6 to 8 slices. Dredge the pieces in the rice flour, patting off the excess.

SEAR

Heat a large skillet over medium-high heat. When it is hot, swirl in enough oil to generously coat the bottom. Arrange the tofu in the pan so the pieces are evenly spaced. They should sizzle the moment they touch the hot oil. (If there is not enough room for all of the tofu, cook it in batches, adding more oil as needed.) Sear the tofu until it is golden brown and crisp on the first side, 2 to 3 minutes, then flip, reduce the heat slightly, and brown the second side. Transfer the tofu to a clean platter or individual plates. Or, if you want the tofu to remain crisp on all sides, put it on a baking rack and keep it in a warm oven while you make the sauce, then plate it.

> continues on next page

SAUCE

Discard the frying oil and remove any unappealing brown bits or residue. (Unlike meat or seafood, tofu doesn't leave a flavorful fond.) Let the pan cool slightly, then return it to medium heat and pour in the soy sauce, sugar, and mirin. Bring to a simmer, stirring to dissolve the sugar, and simmer until the sauce just clings to the spoon, about 1 minute. Cook it a bit longer if you'd like a stickier sauce.

Spoon the sauce over the tofu, garnish with the scallion greens, and serve.

Basted Eggs with Asparagus Brown Butter Sauce and Shaved Parmesan

My version of basted eggs might be better described as pan-steamed. There is no need to actually baste them as they cook—I just add a little water and pop a lid on the pan for a minute. The asparagus needs to be thinly sliced so it can be cooked through before the eggs get cold.

THIS SAUCE ALSO GOES WELL WITH: sole, salmon, and chicken or turkey scallopini (refer to the tables on pages 208–26 for cooking tips).

YIELD: 1 SERVING

2 large eggs

1½ tablespoons unsalted butter, cut into 4 equal pieces

1 tablespoon minced bacon or pancetta (optional)

1 tablespoon minced shallot

1 tablespoon water

¼ cup thinly sliced asparagus

1 tablespoon dry white wine, such as Sauvignon Blanc or Pinot Gris (optional)

Salt and finely ground black or white pepper

A small chunk of Parmigiano-Reggiano or similar aged cheese for shaving

PREP

Crack the eggs into a small bowl. This will make them easier to slip into the skillet at the perfect time.

Heat a small lidded skillet over medium heat (nonstick is fine). Add one piece of the butter. When it has melted, add the bacon, if using, and shallot and sauté until the bacon is just turning golden brown and the shallots are tender, about 2 minutes. Nudge the solids towards the edges of the pan and slide the eggs into the pan. When the edges just start to bubble and turn white, splash in the water, cover, and cook the eggs to your preference. Yolks that are just set will take about 1 minute.

SAUCE

Transfer the eggs to a plate. Put the remaining butter in the skillet and cook until it is a nutty brown. Add the asparagus and sauté until it is just tender but still has a nice crunch. Add the wine and simmer until the aroma of raw alcohol has cooked off. Season with salt and pepper.

Pour the asparagus and butter over the eggs. Use a vegetable peeler to shave a few paper-thin slices of cheese over the eggs and serve immediately.

Sunny-Side-Up Eggs with Turmeric Tomato Oil

Sunny-Side-Up Eggs
with Turmeric Tomato Oil

Every time I make these eggs, I'm convinced they are the perfect meal. Enjoy them in your pajamas on a leisurely weekend morning or serve them after a long day with a chunk of rustic bread and glass of white wine. Be sure to scatter the tomatoes into the oil rather than on the eggs so they get warm and saucy.

THIS SAUCE ALSO GOES WELL WITH: rockfish, chicken breast tenderloins, whole small fish, and tofu (refer to the tables on pages 208–26 for cooking tips).

YIELD: 1 SERVING

2 tablespoons extra-virgin olive oil
1 teaspoon finely grated fresh turmeric
  or ¼ teaspoon dried turmeric
2 large eggs
2 to 3 tablespoons minced tomato
Salt and finely ground black pepper
Pinch of cayenne pepper
1 tablespoon minced fresh chives
  or thinly sliced scallion greens

Heat a small skillet over medium-high heat (nonstick is fine here). When it is hot, add the oil and turmeric. Crack the eggs into the pan. When the eggs are half-cooked, sprinkle the tomatoes into the oil around the eggs and season with salt and pepper. Continue to cook the eggs sunny-side up. Or, if you prefer them cooked firmer, pop a lid on the pan and let them steam to your preference.

Use a slotted spatula to slide the eggs onto a plate, then drizzle the sauce over the top. Sprinkle with the cayenne pepper and chives and serve.

Seared Portobello Mushrooms with Stroganoff Sauce

I describe this dish as "upside-down Stroganoff" because instead of beef in a mushroom-rich gravy, it's mushrooms with a beef-nuanced sauce. It has all of the savory and satisfying elements of the classic preparation—melted onions, the pungency of Dijon, and a finish of sour cream—but it is lighter and quicker to fix. Beef stock adds depth and body to the gravy, but for vegetarians, a concentrated brown vegetable or mushroom stock is a good substitute. I like to slice the onions, so they are a feature, but you can mince them or even strain the sauce if you prefer a smoother one. I serve this with noodles as an entrée, but it also makes a good side dish.

THIS SAUCE ALSO GOES WELL WITH: ground beef or bison patties, steaks, chicken, meatballs, and calf's liver (refer to the tables on pages 208–26 for cooking tips).

YIELD: 2 ENTRÉE SERVINGS OR 4 SIDES

2 tablespoons clarified
  butter or neutral oil
4 large (4-inch/10-cm) portobello
  mushroom caps
1 cup low-sodium beef, mushroom,
  or brown vegetable stock,
  preferably homemade
1 cup sliced yellow onion
1 clove garlic, chopped
1 teaspoon paprika (hot or mild)
¼ cup dry white wine, such as
  Sauvignon Blanc or Pinot Gris
½ teaspoon kosher salt, or to taste
Freshly ground black pepper
¼ cup sour cream
1 tablespoon Dijon mustard
1 tablespoon Worcestershire sauce
1 tablespoon chopped
  fresh dill or tarragon

SEAR

Heat a large lidded sauté pan over medium heat. When it is hot, swirl in just enough clarified butter to coat the bottom. Arrange the mushroom caps, rounded side down, in the pan so they are evenly spaced. Sear until they are a light golden brown, about 2 minutes. They will not develop a lot of color, and they will brown only at the peaks, unless you roll them, but even a little color will add flavor. Do not press on the mushrooms to flatten them, or they will crack. Flip the mushrooms over and remove the pan from the heat.

Let the pan cool for a minute (the surface will be extremely hot) and then, being careful to protect your hands and face from the steam, pour in half the stock and immediately cover with the lid to trap the steam. Return the pan to medium heat and simmer until the mushrooms are warmed through but still firm, about 2 minutes. Transfer the mushrooms and cooking liquid to a shallow dish and set aside.

SAUCE

Return the pan to medium heat. Add the remaining butter and sauté the onions, stirring often, until soft and golden brown, 6 to 7 minutes. Add the garlic and sauté until the aroma blooms, about 20 seconds. Stir in the paprika, then deglaze the pan with the wine. Use a wooden spoon to dissolve any brown residue on the bottom of the pan. Simmer until the raw aroma of alcohol is gone and the volume is reduced by about half. Add the remaining stock, the mushrooms, and all of the collected juices, season with the salt and with pepper to taste, and simmer, uncovered, until the juices are dark and reduced by about half.

While the mushrooms are simmering, stir together the sour cream, mustard, and Worcestershire in a small bowl.

Remove the pan from the heat and use a slotted spoon or spatula to lift the mushrooms onto a clean platter or individual plates. Temper the sour cream mixture by stirring in some of the hot pan liquid a tablespoon at a time until it is warm and fluid, then pour it into the skillet and heat gently. Do not boil the sauce after the sour cream has been added. Taste and adjust the seasoning with salt and pepper if needed.

Spoon the sauce over the mushroom caps, sprinkle with the herbs, and serve.

Ingredients for Portobello Mushroom Caps with Marmite Gravy: portobello mushrooms, Marmite, fresh thyme

Portobello Mushroom Caps with Marmite Gravy

I once described the super-concentrated umami flavor of Marmite as being the vegetarian equivalent of the sticky stuff at the bottom of a roast beef pan. That's when it hit me—why not use Marmite to make vegetarian brown gravy? A little bit of Marmite goes a long way. The intensity can be slightly off-putting: Use just enough to highlight the salty, savory, yeasty flavors, but not so much that it seems shocking or bitter. I consider this dish the meatless equivalent of steak and gravy.

 THIS SAUCE ALSO GOES WELL WITH: English sausages, beef or buffalo patties, and calf's liver (refer to the tables on pages 208–26 for cooking tips).

YIELD: 2 ENTRÉE SERVINGS OR 4 SIDES

2 teaspoons Marmite

1½ cups boiling water

3 tablespoons neutral oil or clarified butter

4 large (4-inch/10-cm) portobello mushroom caps

2 tablespoons all-purpose flour

1 teaspoon chopped fresh thyme or ¼ teaspoon dried thyme

1 teaspoon tomato paste

Salt and freshly ground black pepper

PREP

Stir together the Marmite and boiling water in a small bowl to make a quick "mock stock."

SEAR

Heat a large lidded sauté pan over medium heat. Swirl in just enough oil to coat the bottom. Arrange the mushroom caps, rounded side down, in the pan so they are evenly spaced. Sear until they are a light golden brown, about 2 minutes. They will not develop a lot of color, and they will only brown at the peaks unless you roll them, but even a little color will add flavor. Do not press on the mushrooms to flatten them, or they will crack. Flip the mushrooms, reduce the heat slightly, and brown the other side, about 2 minutes.

Let the pan cool for a minute (the surface will be very hot) and then, being careful to protect your hands and face from the steam, pour in half the Marmite stock and immediately cover the pan with the lid to trap the steam. Return the pan to medium heat and simmer until the mushrooms are warmed through but still firm, about 2 minutes. Transfer the mushrooms and cooking liquid to a shallow dish and set aside.

> continues on next page

SAUCE

Return the pan to medium heat and add the remaining oil. When it is hot, remove the skillet from the heat, sprinkle in the flour, and stir into a smooth paste. (Removing the pan from the heat helps ensure that the lumps are all smoothed out before the roux starts to cook.) Return the pan to medium heat and cook, stirring constantly, until the roux turns a dark, nutty brown, about 4 minutes. Brown roux is used as a flavoring, not just a thickener, so make sure it is nice and toasty. Whisk in the thyme, tomato paste, the remaining Marmite stock, and the mushroom cooking juices and stir until the sauce thickens into a classic gravy consistency. It will look, smell, and taste fine at this point, but simmering it for an additional 10 minutes will improve the flavor and texture.

Taste and adjust the seasoning with salt and pepper. Although the umami intensity of the Marmite can mimic salt, a pinch of salt will actually balance out the flavors. Nestle the mushrooms into the gravy and warm until they are reheated, a minute or two, then lift them onto a serving platter or individual plates.

Spoon some gravy over the top of the mushrooms and serve with the rest in a gravy boat alongside.

Seared Tomato Halves with Crispy Garlic Oil

The success of this recipe depends on the quality of the tomatoes. It is perfect on hot midsummer nights. While I don't usually like browned garlic, in this case the nutty aroma and crisp texture of lightly toasted garlic adds a lot to the dish. Serve these as an entrée or side dish with thick slices of toasted rustic bread.

THIS SAUCE ALSO GOES WELL WITH: tuna steaks, beef steaks, shrimp, broccoli, calamari steaks, and split lobster tails (refer to the tables on pages 208–26 for cooking tips).

YIELD: 2 ENTRÉE SERVINGS OR 4 SIDES

2 medium-sized ripe tomatoes

1 tablespoon neutral or olive oil

2 to 3 tablespoons dry white wine, such as Sauvignon Blanc or Pinot Gris

3 tablespoons extra-virgin olive oil

3 to 4 cloves garlic, sliced

Pinch of red chile flakes

Salt and freshly ground black pepper

PREP

Core the tomatoes and cut them horizontally in half. Remove some of the juice and seeds by gently squeezing the halves and shaking them. Removing the extra liquid will help the tomatoes brown. Pat the cut surfaces of the tomatoes dry with paper towels.

SEAR

Heat a large skillet over medium-high heat—a well-seasoned cast-iron skillet works particularly well for this. When the pan is hot, swirl in just enough oil to coat the bottom. Arrange the tomatoes, cut side down, in the pan so they are evenly spaced. They should sizzle the moment they contact the hot oil. Leave the tomatoes alone until you can clearly see the bottom edges brown and start to char, about 2 minutes; they should be warmed through but not collapsing; they will continue to soften slightly as they rest. Lift the tomatoes out of the pan with a thin spatula, maintaining as much of the dark crust as you can, and arrange them browned side up on a serving dish or individual plates.

> *continues on next page*

SAUCE

Deglaze the pan with the white wine and simmer until the aroma of raw alcohol is gone. Pour the deglazing liquid over the tomatoes.

Wipe the pan clean and return it to medium heat. Swirl in the extra-virgin olive oil, garlic, and red chile flakes and cook, stirring often, until the garlic is golden brown and slightly toasted, no more than a minute. The garlic can go from golden to scorched in an instant, so watch it carefully. (If it burns, start again with fresh oil and garlic.)

Spoon the garlic and oil over the tomatoes. Sprinkle generously with salt and pepper and serve.

Seared Tomato Halves with Crispy Garlic Oil (page 185)

Pan-Toasted Rustic Bread with clarified butter

Pan-Toasted Rustic Bread with Swiss Cheese and Wine Sauce

Think of this as fondue for two, without those silly forks. This isn't a sauce you can fiddle with. You need to heat it through, slide it onto the toasted bread, and then serve it immediately, or it can separate or seize up. The cornstarch helps stabilize the cheese. I tried omitting it, but the texture was never as consistent. The taste isn't noticeable, especially if you use a good cheese.

For a bit more flair, scatter the top of the bread with chopped cornichons, pickled onions, diced tomatoes, or slivers of cured meat, like a wine salami, guanciale, or speck. If you have it and are feeling traditional, go ahead and stir a teaspoon of Kirsch into the cheese sauce right before serving.

💡 **THIS SAUCE ALSO GOES WELL WITH:** smoked sausages, pork, chicken , broccoli, and polenta cakes (refer to the tables on pages 208–26 for cooking tips).

YIELD: 2 SERVINGS

2 thick slices rustic bread

About 1 tablespoon olive oil or clarified butter

½ cup dry white wine, such as Sauvignon Blanc or Pinot Gris

1 clove garlic, mashed to a paste

4 ounces (115 g) Swiss cheese, such as Gruyère, Emmenthaler, Appenzeller, and/or raclette, grated

¼ teaspoon cornstarch

PREP

Brush both sides of the bread lightly with the oil.

SEAR

Heat a medium skillet over medium heat. When it is hot, arrange the bread in the pan and press lightly on it so there is as much surface contact as possible, then slowly toast the bread until it is dark brown but not burnt on the first side, 3 to 4 minutes. Flip and toast the other side. Transfer the bread to two plates.

SAUCE

Remove the pan from the heat and let cool slightly, or the wine will evaporate almost instantly. Wipe out any oil or brown bits. Pour in the wine, add the garlic, return the pan to medium heat, and simmer until the raw aroma of alcohol is gone.

While the wine is reducing, toss the cheese with the cornstarch.

Add the cheese mixture to the pan and stir until the cheese is completely melted and the sauce is cohesive and smooth; do not boil. Pour the sauce over the bread and serve immediately.

Seared Eggplant with Walnut and Roasted Red Pepper Puree

The ingredients in this dish are so well suited to one another, I swear they can be combined in virtually any ratio. Here the sauce components are simply whirred until smooth in a blender, then simmered and poured over seared eggplant slices. Try not to use too much oil when you are cooking the eggplant, or the dish can seem heavy or greasy. That said, go ahead and showcase your very best olive oil as a finishing drizzle. Harissa is a Tunisian hot pepper paste and a staple throughout the Mediterranean. Look for it in the specialty foods aisle (if you can't get it, you can substitute red chile flakes).

THIS SAUCE ALSO GOES WELL WITH: lamb chops; lamb, beef, or turkey patties; chicken; calamari steaks; and black cod (refer to the tables on pages 208–26 for cooking tips).

YIELD: 4 SERVINGS

1 cup chopped roasted red peppers
½ cup walnut halves and
    pieces, toasted
⅓ cup chopped yellow onion
5 to 6 cloves garlic, chopped
2 teaspoons harissa, or to taste
    (or substitute 1 teaspoon
    red chile flakes)
1½ teaspoons fresh thyme leaves
    or ½ teaspoon dried thyme
1 teaspoon ground cumin
2 teaspoons kosher salt, or to taste
½ teaspoon freshly ground
    black pepper, or to taste
About 3 tablespoons olive oil
1 large eggplant, sliced
    into 6 to 8 rounds
About 2 tablespoons freshly
    squeezed lemon juice
    > continues on next page

PREP

Make the pepper puree: Combine the roasted peppers, most of the walnuts (save about 2 tablespoons for garnish) the onion, garlic, harissa, thyme, cumin, salt, and pepper in a blender or food processor and puree until smooth. Set aside.

SEAR

Heat a large skillet over medium-high heat. When the pan is hot, swirl in just enough oil to coat the bottom with a thin film. Arrange 3 or 4 slices of eggplant in the pan. They should sizzle when they touch the oil. Sear to a golden brown on the first side, about 4 minutes, then flip, add a bit more oil if necessary, and cook until the eggplant is brown on the second side and just soft. It will continue to soften slightly as it rests. Transfer the slices to a platter and keep warm while you repeat the process for the remaining eggplant.

Extra-virgin olive oil for drizzling

⅓ cup crumbled fresh goat cheese or similar tangy cheese

2 tablespoons coarsely chopped fresh mint

SAUCE

Discard the cooking oil and wipe the pan clean. Cool the skillet slightly, then return it to medium heat. Add any remaining oil, pour in the pepper puree, and bring to a simmer. Cook until the puree has darkened slightly and there is no raw onion or garlic flavor, about 3 minutes. The puree should be the consistency of thick gravy. Stir in the lemon juice. Taste and adjust the seasoning with salt, pepper, and/or harissa if you like.

Dollop the sauce evenly over the eggplant and drizzle with extra-virgin olive oil. Garnish with the crumbled cheese, reserved walnuts, and chopped mint. Serve hot or at room temperature.

Ingredients for Sweet Potato Planks with Orange Maple Glaze: sweet potato, yam, maple syrup, and orange halves

Sweet Potato Planks
with Orange Maple Glaze

Sweet potato or yam planks cook quite quickly, brown well, and are hearty enough to carry sturdy sauces. They can be served as a main course or side dish. This sauce couldn't be much simpler; it's a jazzed-up juice reduction. I like it with plenty of cayenne pepper. The starchy sweet potatoes can take a lot of spice. For the best planks, choose sweet potatoes that are straight and evenly shaped.

THIS SAUCE ALSO GOES WELL WITH: salmon, turkey scaloppini, shrimp, and ham steaks (refer to the tables on pages 208–26 for cooking tips).

YIELD: 1 ENTRÉE SERVING OR 2 TO 4 SIDES

1 large (10 to 12 ounces/285 to 340 g) sweet potato or yam
1 tablespoon neutral oil or clarified butter
½ cup orange juice, preferably freshly squeezed
1 teaspoon finely grated orange zest
1 tablespoon pure maple syrup, or to taste
¼ teaspoon kosher salt, or to taste
Pinch of cayenne pepper, or to taste
1 tablespoon cold unsalted butter (optional)
Freshly ground black pepper

PREP

Scrub the sweet potato well and slice it lengthwise into planks no thicker than ½ inch/1 cm.

SEAR

Heat a large skillet over medium heat. When it is hot, swirl in the oil. Arrange the potato slices in the pan so they are evenly spaced. (The high sugar content of the potatoes makes them susceptible to burning, so, unlike many of the recipes in this book, the pieces do not need to audibly sizzle when they are added to the hot oil.) Cook the potatoes until they are golden brown on the first side, 3 to 4 minutes. Flip and brown the other side, then continue to cook, flipping often, until the potatoes are just fork-tender, about 6 minutes longer. They will continue to cook slightly as they rest. Lift the potato planks onto a platter and blot them dry if they seem oily.

> continues on next page

SAUCE

Discard the cooking oil. Deglaze the pan with the orange juice. Use a wooden spoon to soften and dissolve any brown residue on the bottom of the pan. Add the orange zest, maple syrup, salt, and cayenne pepper and simmer until the sauce is reduced to a clinging, slightly sticky glaze.

Add the butter, if using, and stir to melt it evenly into the sauce. Taste the sauce and adjust the seasoning as needed with salt and black pepper, and more cayenne and/or syrup if you like. The potatoes are starchy, so the sauce should be strongly flavored.

Drizzle the sauce over the potatoes and serve.

Charred Broccoli with Chile, Garlic, and Lemon Oil

Infused oils can be made by simply warming flavorings in a good-quality oil. They are quick and sturdy, and they carry bold flavors well. The trick is to make sure the oil and aromatics or other flavorings don't burn. My favorite oil for searing or stir-frying vegetables is peanut oil, but I am becoming more enamored of rice bran oil and raw sesame oil. Charring the broccoli is a smoky, aromatic process, but the added flavor is worth it.

Taste the chiles when you are slicing them so you can judge their heat. If they are fiery, use less; if they are mild, boost the heat with a pinch of red chile flakes.

THIS SAUCE ALSO GOES WELL WITH: shrimp, snapper, small steaks, and tofu (refer to the tables on pages 208–26 for cooking tips).

YIELD: 4 SERVINGS

1 to 1½ pounds (450 to 675 g) broccoli—choose compact heads with long, thick stems
1 small lemon
About ⅓ cup peanut oil, rice bran oil, or raw sesame oil
2 to 3 tablespoons water or low-sodium chicken stock, preferably homemade
½ teaspoon kosher salt, or to taste
Freshly ground black pepper
3 cloves garlic, sliced
1 to 2 medium-hot red chiles, such as Fresno, red jalapeño, or Holland, seeded and thinly sliced, or to taste

PREP

To prepare the broccoli, run a vegetable peeler from the flower end down the stem of each stalk. The stem doesn't need to be peeled perfectly, but it is more appealing when the tough skin is removed. For the broccoli to brown, it needs as much contact with the pan as possible, so cut large, flat pieces if you can. Leaving the stems in place makes the pieces easier to flip. Pat the broccoli dry.

Use a vegetable peeler to remove the lemon zest in strips, then cut the strips into fine slivers (or use a lemon zester). Squeeze the juice from the lemon and set aside.

SEAR

Heat a large lidded sauté pan over medium-high heat—cast iron is a good choice for this if you have a lid that fits the pan. When the pan is hot, swirl in just enough oil to coat the bottom. Arrange some of the broccoli in a single layer, trying to make as much surface contact with the pan as you can. (You will need to cook the broccoli in batches, wiping the pan clean and adding fresh oil as needed.) Leave the broccoli untouched until you start to see a

> *continues on next page*

wisp of smoke rising and smell it starting to char, about 2 minutes. When the pieces have developed some distinctive blackened spots, flip them and cook for another minute. Lift the broccoli onto a plate and repeat with the remaining pieces. (The broccoli will not be cooked through at this point.)

Return all of the broccoli to the skillet, add the water, immediately cover the pan with the lid, and let the broccoli steam for about 1 minute. It should be just fork-tender but still vibrantly green. Transfer the broccoli to a platter. Use kitchen shears to trim the stems or cut the pieces into smaller florets if you like. Sprinkle with the salt and pepper to taste.

SAUCE

Add the remaining oil (3 to 4 tablespoons), the garlic, chiles, and lemon zest to the skillet. Cook until the garlic is just barely golden brown, about 1 minute. Add the lemon juice and adjust the seasoning with salt and pepper as needed.

Drizzle or spoon the sauce over the broccoli, lifting and turning the pieces to coat. Serve immediately.

Charred Broccoli with Chile, Garlic, and Lemon Oil (page 195)

Pan-Seared Provolone "Steaks"
with Warm Cherry Tomatoes

Pan-Seared Provolone "Steaks" with Warm Cherry Tomatoes

On a trip to Argentina, my husband and I were served thick slabs of aged provolone cheese that had been grilled over hot coals until they were crusted brown on the outside and just soft inside. The cheese was knife-and-fork tender, slightly chewy, and perfect with crusty bread. I thought I would try making something similar in a hot skillet and I found that a well-seasoned cast-iron pan browns the cheese beautifully. It can take a bit of finesse to flip the provolone—you don't want to leave the cheese crust attached to the pan. A thin flexible spatula works best. Have your cheesemonger slice the cheese into even "steaks" for you.

THIS SAUCE ALSO GOES WELL WITH: salmon, fresh sardines, eggplant, steaks, and chicken (all cooked through before saucing; refer to the tables on pages 208–26 for cooking tips).

YIELD: 2 ENTRÉE SERVINGS OR 4 SIDES

About 1 tablespoon neutral oil

8 ounces (225 g) provolone, preferably aged, cut into 2 thick (½-inch/1.25-cm) rounds

2 tablespoons extra-virgin olive oil

1 cup quartered cherry tomatoes (about 6 ounces/170 g)

2 cloves garlic, chopped

¼ teaspoon red chile flakes, or to taste

¼ teaspoon dried oregano

Salt and freshly ground black pepper

SEAR

Heat a large heavy skillet over medium-high heat; cast iron is a good choice. When it is hot, swirl in just enough neutral oil to coat the bottom. Place the pieces of cheese in the pan; try not to move them once they touch the hot skillet. Let the cheese brown and form a dark crust on the bottom; about 3 minutes. Carefully slip a thin spatula under the crust and quickly flip the cheese onto a warm platter or individual plates. It shouldn't be completely melted. It will continue to soften while you make the sauce.

SAUCE

Discard the cooking oil and wipe the pan clean. Swirl in the olive oil, add the tomatoes, and stir until they are heated through. Add the garlic, chile flakes, oregano, and salt and pepper to taste and sauté until the tomatoes are soft and juicy, about 1 minute. Taste and adjust the seasoning with salt, pepper, and/or chile flakes.

Pour the tomato sauce over the cheese and serve immediately.

Polenta Cakes with Parmesan Cream Sauce and Shredded Radicchio

To make polenta cakes, you need leftover or cold polenta. For purists, that means making the polenta ahead and chilling it thoroughly, perhaps overnight. A better alternative for a weeknight is to buy a log of polenta at the store and just slice it up. That's what I do. The sauce is basically what people think of as Alfredo sauce. The bitter crunch of the shredded radicchio is a nice counter to the super-rich, creamy sauce.

THIS SAUCE ALSO GOES WELL WITH: chicken, meatballs, salmon, and broccoli (refer to the tables on pages 208–26 for cooking tips).

YIELD: 4 SERVINGS

1 cylinder (16 to 18 ounces/450 to 510 g) precooked polenta, sliced into ½-inch (1.25-cm)-thick rounds

3 to 4 tablespoons olive oil, neutral oil, or clarified butter

1 tablespoon unsalted butter

2 cloves garlic, minced

¾ cup heavy cream

⅓ cup finely grated Parmigiano-Reggiano or similar cheese, plus additional for serving

Salt and finely ground white pepper (optional)

A few gratings of nutmeg

½ cup shredded radicchio

PREP

Pat the polenta slices dry with paper towels.

SEAR

Heat a large skillet over medium heat. (Since polenta has a tendency to stick, and it doesn't leave any fond, this is one of the rare situations where I can recommend a nonstick skillet.) When the pan is hot, swirl in enough oil to generously coat the bottom. Arrange the polenta cakes in the pan so they are evenly spaced. If necessary, cook them in batches, wiping the pan clean and adding fresh oil as needed. Fry the cakes until they are brown and crispy on the first side, 4 to 5 minutes, then flip and cook until browned on the second side, about 4 minutes. Transfer the polenta to a serving dish, or if you want to keep the cakes crisp, place them on a wire rack and keep warm in a low oven while you make the sauce.

SAUCE

Cool the pan slightly, then discard the cooking oil and any unappealing brown bits. Return the skillet to medium heat and add the butter. When it is melted and foamy, add the garlic and sauté until the aroma blooms, about 20 seconds. Pour in the cream, increase the heat, and bring to a simmer. Cook, stirring often, until the cream is thickened and reduced by about half. Stir in the cheese until it is just melted; do not boil the sauce after the cheese has been added. Add the nutmeg. Taste and adjust the seasoning, keeping in mind that the cheese will have made the sauce quite salty.

Spoon the sauce over the polenta to coat it evenly. Scatter the radicchio over the top and serve. Pass additional cheese at the table so diners can help themselves.

IMPROVISING

Deglazing a skillet for It's-Been-a-Long-Damn-Day-Wine-from-Your-Glass Pan Sauce (page 206)

Brainstorming

ONCE YOU HAVE A FEEL FOR THE RHYTHM OF SEARING FOODS AND MAKING FRESH pan sauces, it's time to start improvising and creating your own recipes. I have put together some ideas here to help with brainstorming and execution; see the recipe and charts that follow. The quantities in the charts are general estimates for a single pan sauce. You will have to make adjustments to suit your own tastes and ingredient choices.

Peruse your cupboards and refrigerator shelves for specialty foods and seasonal ingredients. You might find a use for that last spoonful of capers or fig jam, or a dollop of Peruvian yellow pepper paste. Is your chive plant busting out of the pot? Add a handful of sliced chives to your simple butter sauce, and it will taste like springtime.

Please start simply, with proven taste combinations. Unbridled creativity is great, but it's helpful to remember that when you mix all the colors in your paint box together, you always end up with a strange brown. Also remember that the flavor of the sauce must work in tandem with the main ingredient. No matter how proud you are of a sauce that features a French rosé, fresh nectarines, and lavender, it doesn't belong anywhere near a skirt steak.

It's-Been-a-Long-Damn-Day-
Wine-from-Your-Glass Pan Sauce

This recipe was included in my last book, *Mastering Sauces*. Readers chuckled, then drilled me for more information. "That's how I want to cook!" Essentially, this entire book stems from a basic recipe framework: Sear. Deglaze. Embellish. Once you've cooked your way through some of the recipes, you will know how diverse and adaptable the technique is. And you'll see dinner potential in ingredients you previously overlooked. Whenever you need a refresher, use this framework as a guideline.

I will boldly assume that if you are enjoying a glass of wine with dinner, you have chosen something taste-appropriate to your ingredients. If not, you will need to pour from another bottle. If you're not sure, go ahead and stick with the accepted generalizations: reds with dark meats, whites with lighter meats and seafood; rosés are generally best left in the glass. Of course there are always exceptions. The more you learn about food-and-wine pairing, the more pleasure you will have mixing and matching wines in pan sauces. Ales and hard cider also make good pan sauces, but they tend to need more concentration to become as flavorful as wine. Stocks, broths, and some juices can also work.

PREP

Choose a quick-cooking entrée like boneless chicken, thin steaks, fish fillets, shrimp, or firm tofu. Pat dry and season generously with salt and pepper. Dredge lightly in flour if the food is wet or soft, like tender fish fillets.

SEAR

Heat a large skillet over medium-high heat. When it is hot, swirl in enough oil or clarified butter to just coat the bottom. Arrange the food in the pan so the pieces are evenly spaced. They should each sizzle as they touch the hot pan. Sear until browned on the first side. Flip. Brown on the other side and then continue cooking, flipping as needed, until just done. If the pieces are very thin and quick-cooking, they may actually be cooked through before the second side is thoroughly browned. If the pieces are thick or uneven, reduce the heat after the first flip and consider a secondary technique like steaming or pan-roasting. (Refer to the tables on pages 208–26 for more specific searing and cooking suggestions.) Lift the cooked food out of the pan onto a clean platter or plates, then remove the pan from the heat if you have not already done so.

ADD AROMATICS

Discard the cooking oil and analyze the pan residue. Remove any burnt residue or unappealing bits. Let the pan cool slightly if it is very hot, and wipe it clean if necessary. Add fresh oil or butter and sauté some aromatics such as minced shallots, onion, garlic, tomatoes, and/or chiles. Do not let them burn.

DEGLAZE

Pour in enough complementary wine, beer, or cider (or juice or good-quality stock) to cover the bottom of the pan. It will instantly bubble and start to evaporate. Use a wooden spoon to soften and dissolve any brown residue. Simmer until the alcohol loses the strong, sharp, "raw" aroma. For a more concentrated, intense sauce, simmer longer. You should end up with about 2 tablespoons of intensely flavored liquid per serving.

EMBELLISH

To enrich a sauce, stir in some cold butter, heavy cream, or good flavorful oil at the end. A teaspoon or two per person is fine. Add additional flavorings or ingredients such as Dijon mustard, chopped fresh herbs, and/or a squeeze of lemon if you like. Taste and adjust the seasoning with salt and pepper as necessary. Return the seared ingredient(s) to the pan to coat with sauce, or simply pour the sauce over your entrée. Serve immediately.

COOKING OILS

TYPE	NOTES
Avocado	High smoke point. Distinctive green color and slight vegetal flavor.
Canola (refined)	Neutral. Inexpensive. Very popular. Avoid oversized containers to prevent rancidity.
Clarified butter/ghee	Rich flavor, aroma, and color. Higher smoke point than whole butter.
Coconut	Assertive flavor. Strong aroma. Low smoke point.
Corn (refined)	Considered neutral but can have a distinctive yellow color and corn aroma. Slightly thicker than other neutral oils.
Duck or chicken fat	Assertive flavor and aroma.
Extra-light olive	Light color, neutral flavor. More suitable for higher-temperature cooking than extra-virgin olive oil.
Extra-virgin olive	Can be strongly flavored. Varies greatly by region and brand. Low smoke point. Best saved for recipes that are enhanced by the taste of olives.
Grapeseed	Mildly flavored. High smoke point. Very green color.
Lard	Assertive flavor and aroma. Browns meats particularly well. Remains flavorful even after smoke point has been reached.
Peanut (refined)	Considered neutral, but some brands are quite flavorful and aromatic. High smoke point.
Rice Bran	Neutral. Very versatile. Maintains a relatively clean flavor even after smoke point has been reached.
Safflower (refined)	Neutral. Inexpensive. The highest smoke point of the neutral oils.
Sesame (raw, semi-refined)	Neutral. High smoke point. (Do not confuse with toasted sesame oil, which is dark and strongly flavored.)
Soybean (refined)	Neutral. Inexpensive.
Sunflower (refined)	Neutral. Similar to safflower oil but has a slightly lower smoke point.
Vegetable (refined)	Neutral. Often made with a blend of oils such as safflower, soy, and canola, so characteristics can vary by brand.

FISH AND SEAFOOD

INGREDIENT	Average Raw Weight (or unit) PER PERSON	BASIC SEARING TECHNIQUE
Fish Fillets, *with or without skin* (salmon, cod, halibut, mackerel, sea bass, catfish, or rockfish)	4 to 8 oz./115 to 225 g	Dredge in flour if desired. Sear over medium to medium-high heat until golden brown, carefully flip, and cook through in the skillet, pan-roast in a hot oven, or simmer in sauce until the flakes at the thickest point have loosened but the fish remains moist. The fish will continue to cook slightly as it rests. *Fond: none to medium*
Firm Fish Steaks, *boneless, skinless* (tuna, swordfish, or sturgeon)	3 to 5 oz./85 to 140 g	Fish steaks that are meant to be cooked through should be seared over medium-high heat, flipping regularly, until flaky, or finished by pan-roasting or simmering in sauce. First sear both sides of the fish over medium-high heat. Then, if more cooking is needed, reduce the heat slightly and continue to flip regularly in the skillet, or pan-roast in a hot oven or simmer in sauce, until the fish starts to flake at the thickest point. For sashimi-grade fish served rare to medium-rare, sear over high heat just until browned on all sides. *Fond: light*
Whole Small Fish, *scaled, gutted, and trimmed* (fresh sardines, smelt, pompano, butterfish, trout, or mackerel)	Up to 1 lb./450 g	Cut a few slashes in the sides of thicker or larger fish to help them cook evenly. Dredge in flour. Sear over medium heat, then continue to cook over reduced heat, flipping often, or pan-roast in a medium-hot oven, or simmer in sauce until the flesh at the thickest point is just starting to flake. *Fond: varies according to size and fat content*
Shrimp, *medium to large, headless, peeled, and deveined*	4 to 6 oz./115 to 170 g	Sear over medium-high to high heat, making sure there is plenty of space between the shrimp. Flip and cook until just curled, pink, and firm. *Fond: medium*
Sea Scallops, *large*	3 or 4 scallops	Sear over medium-high to high heat, making sure there is plenty of space between the scallops. Flip, reduce the temperature slightly and cook until just barely firm. *Fond: medium*
Crab, Dungeness, *cleaned and cracked*	½ crab	Sauté or simmer in sauce. Cooked crabs just need to be heated through. Uncooked crabs should be cooked until the flesh is opaque and can slip from the shells. *Fond: none to light*

> continues on next page

FISH AND SEAFOOD

INGREDIENT	Average Raw Weight (or unit) PER PERSON	BASIC SEARING TECHNIQUE
Crab, soft-shell, *cleaned*	2 crabs	Dredge in flour. Sear in a fair amount of oil or clarified butter until browned and crisp, then flip or pan-roast in a hot oven until just cooked through. *Fond: none*
Lobster Tails, *split*	½ to 1 tail	Sear split side down over medium to medium-high heat until golden brown. Flip and finish cooking by steaming, simmering in sauce, or pan-roasting in a hot oven until just opaque throughout. *Fond: light to medium*
Oysters, *extra-small, shucked*	6 oysters	Drain well. Dredge in flour and sear over medium-high heat until browned. Flip, reduce the heat slightly, and cook to your personal preference, from just warmed through to firm. *Fond: none to light*
Calamari Steaks	1 steak	Dredge in flour. Sear over medium to medium-high heat until browned on both sides. Then continue to cook, flipping regularly, to your desired doneness, from very tender to slightly firm and springy. *Fond: none to light.*
Fish Cakes, Burgers, or Patties	3 to 5 oz./85 to 140 g	Sear over medium-high heat, flipping carefully, until browned on both sides, then reduce the heat to medium and continue to cook, flipping once or twice, until just cooked through. Precooked fish cakes such as Korean *eomuk* can simply be warmed through. *Fond: none to light*

CHICKEN AND POULTRY

INGREDIENT	Average Raw Weight (or unit) PER PERSON	BASIC SEARING TECHNIQUE
Chicken, *boneless, skinless* (breasts, thighs, or breast tenderloins)	6 to 8 oz./170 to 225 g	Pound to an even thickness. Sear over medium-high heat until browned, flip, reduce the heat slightly, and continue to cook, flipping occasionally, until just cooked through (165°F/74°). *Fond: medium*
Chicken, *boneless, skin-on* ("airline" breasts or thighs)	8 to 12 oz./225 to 340 g	Sear skin side down, flip, and pan-roast in a hot oven. Or continue to sear over reduced heat, or simmer in sauce, flipping and turning often, until just cooked through (165°F/74°C). *Fond: medium to dark*
Chicken, *bone-in, skin-on* (breasts, thighs, legs, "drumettes," or chicken quarters)	8 to 12 oz./225 to 340 g	Sear skin side down, flip, and pan-roast in a medium-hot oven. Or continue to sear over reduced heat, or simmer in sauce, flipping and turning often, until cooked through (165°F/74°C). *Fond: medium to dark*
Cornish Hens or Poussins, *split*	½ bird	Sear skin side down, flip, and pan-roast in a medium-hot oven. Or continue to sear over reduced heat, or simmer in sauce, flipping and turning often, until cooked through (165°F/74°C). *Fond: medium to dark*
Quail, *semi-boneless* (with legs and wing bones intact)	1 or 2 quail	Sear breast side down, flip, and pan-roast in a hot oven until cooked to your desired temperature. (The USDA recommends that poultry be cooked to an internal temperature of at least 165°F/74°C, but some chefs prefer that quail be cooked to medium.) *Fond: medium to dark*
Duck Breasts, *skin on, boneless*	1 breast	Place the breasts skin side up on an ice pack to chill the meat for 5 minutes. Cut a crosshatch pattern in the skin and fat. Sear skin side down until browned and crisp, flip, and then pan-roast in a 425°F/218°C oven, flipping every 2 to 3 minutes, until cooked to a few degrees below your desired temperature (see page 17). *Fond: dark*

> continues on next page

CHICKEN AND POULTRY

INGREDIENT	Average Raw Weight (or unit) PER PERSON	BASIC SEARING TECHNIQUE
Turkey Breast, *boneless, skinless* (cutlets or scaloppini)	4 to 6 oz./115 to 170 g	Pound to an even thickness. Sear over medium-high heat, flipping occasionally, until browned on both sides and just cooked through (165°F/74°C). *Fond: medium*
Ground Poultry, *chicken or turkey* (patties, burgers, or meatballs)	4 to 6 oz./115 to 170 g	Sear over medium-high heat, flipping often, until browned, or simmer in sauce until cooked through (165°F/74°C). *Fond: medium*

MEATS

INGREDIENT	Average Raw Weight (or unit) PER PERSON	BASIC SEARING TECHNIQUE
Beef, *thin-cut steaks (½ inch/1.25 cm or under) (petite sirloins, tournedos, or skirt steak)*	4 to 6 oz./60 to 170 g	Sear over medium-high to high heat until dark brown, flip, and cook to just below your personal preference. Thin steaks need minimal cooking on the second side to reach medium-rare. *Fond: medium to dark*
Beef, *average-sized steaks (½ to 1 inch/1.25 to 2.5 cm), boneless or bone-in (sirloin, rib eye, flatiron, or flank)*	4 to 8 oz./115 to 225 g (slightly more for bone-in steaks)	Sear over medium-high heat until browned, flip, reduce the temperature slightly, and cook, flipping regularly, to just a degree or two below your personal preference. Let rest for a few minutes before slicing or serving. *Fond: dark*
Beef, *thick-cut steaks (1 inch/2.5 cm or more), boneless or bone-in (rib steak, NY strip, or tenderloin)*	4 to 8 oz./115 to 225 g (slightly more for bone-in steaks)	Sear over medium-high heat until browned on all sides. Reduce the temperature slightly, and continue to cook, flipping regularly, or pan-roast in a medium-hot oven, until cooked to just a few degrees below your personal preference. Let rest for 5 minutes before slicing or serving. *Fond: dark to very dark*
Beef, *kalbi or cross-cut short ribs*	1 or 2 pieces	Sear over medium-high heat until browned, flip, and continue to cook, or simmer in sauce, flipping occasionally, until cooked to your personal preference. *Fond: dark*
Ground Beef or Buffalo *patties or meatballs*	4 to 6 oz./115 to 170 g	Sear over medium-high heat until browned, flip, and continue to cook, or simmer in sauce, flipping occasionally, until cooked through. *Fond: dark*
Calf's Liver, *cleaned and sliced*	4 to 6 oz./ 115 to 170 g	Dredge in flour. Sear over medium-high heat until browned, then flip, reduce the heat slightly, and cook to your personal preference. *Fond: medium to dark*
Pork, *thin-cut, boneless or bone-in (chops, cutlets, or scaloppini)*	4 to 6 oz./115 to 170 g	Sear over medium-high heat until browned, flip, and cook through. *Fond: medium*
Pork, *average thickness (about ½ inch/1.25 cm), boneless or bone-in (chops or loin slices)*	6 to 10 oz./170 to 285 g bone-in pork; 4 to 6 oz./115 to 170 g boneless pork; or 1 to 2 bone-in chops	Sear over medium-high heat until browned, then flip, reduce the heat slightly, and continue to cook, flipping as needed, or simmer in sauce, until cooked to your personal preference. *Fond: medium to dark*

> continues on next page

MEATS

INGREDIENT	Average Raw Weight (or unit) PER PERSON	BASIC SEARING TECHNIQUE
Pork, *thick-cut (more than ½ inch/1.25 cm), boneless or bone-in (rib or loin chops)*	1 chop (less if they are very large and can be sliced to serve)	Sear over medium-high heat until browned on all sides. Reduce the heat and continue to cook, flipping regularly, or pan-roast in a hot oven, or simmer in sauce, until cooked to a degree or two below your personal preference. Let rest for a few minutes before serving. *Fond: dark*
Pork Tenderloin, *whole small*	4 to 6 oz./115 to 170 g	Sear over medium-high heat until browned on all sides. Then pan-roast in a hot oven until cooked to a degree or two below your desired doneness. Let rest for a few minutes before slicing. *Fond: medium to dark*
Ground Pork, *patties, bulk sausage, or meatballs*	4 to 5 oz./115 to 140 g	Sear over medium-high heat until browned, then flip and continue cooking, or simmer in sauce, flipping occasionally, until cooked through. *Fond: medium to dark*
Sausages, *fresh, in casings (sweet or hot Italian, bratwurst, bangers, merguez, or boerewors)*	4 to 5 oz./115 to 140 g	Sear over medium heat until browned on all sides. Reduce the heat and continue to cook, or steam or simmer, until cooked through. *Fond: medium*
Sausages, *cured or smoked (kielbasa, smoked German, or frankfurters)*	4 to 5 oz./115 to 140 g	Sear, whole or sliced, until browned on all sides, or simmer in sauce until heated through. *Fond: medium*
Sausage, *patties or meatballs*	4 to 5 oz./115 to 170 g	Sear over medium-high heat until browned, then flip and continue cooking, or simmer in sauce, flipping occasionally, until cooked through. *Fond: medium*
Ham, slice or steaks, *fully cooked, bone-in or boneless; country ham slices should be properly de-salinated*	3 to 5 oz./85 to 140 g	Sear over medium-high heat until browned on both sides, or simmer in sauce until heated through. *Fond: medium*
Lamb, *loin chops*	2 chops	Sear over medium-high heat until browned on both sides. Reduce the heat and continue to cook, flipping often, or pan-roast in a medium-hot oven, until cooked to your personal preference. Let rest for a few minutes before serving. *Fond: dark to very dark*

MEATS

INGREDIENT	Average Raw Weight (or unit) PER PERSON	BASIC SEARING TECHNIQUE
Lamb, *"rack"* (rib chops)	3 or 4 chops each	Sear over medium-high heat until browned on all sides, then flip, reduce the heat to medium, and continue to cook, or pan-roast in a hot oven, until cooked to just a few degrees below your personal preference. Let rest for a few minutes before slicing into chops and serving. *Fond: dark to very dark*
Lamb, *steaks* (leg steaks)	6 to 8 oz./170 to 225 g	Sear over medium-high heat until browned, then flip, reduce the heat slightly, and continue to cook, flipping often, or simmer in sauce, until cooked to your personal preference. *Fond: dark*
Ground Lamb, *patties, burgers, or meatballs*	4 to 6 oz./115 to 170 g	Sear over medium-high heat until browned on both sides, then reduce the heat to medium and continue to cook, flipping regularly, or simmer in sauce, until cooked through. *Fond: dark*
Veal *scallopini*	3 to 4 oz./85 to 115 g	Dredge in flour. Sear over medium-high heat until golden brown on the first side, flip, and cook until just pink inside. The meat may be done before the second side is completely browned. *Fond: light to medium*
Game and Specialty Meats, *steaks, cutlets, boneless breasts, ground meat, or sausage*	3 to 6 oz./85 to 170 g	Varies. See instructions for similar cuts of beef

VEGETARIAN

INGREDIENT	Average Raw Weight (or unit) PER PERSON	BASIC SEARING TECHNIQUE
Tofu, *firm*	4 to 8 oz./115 to 225 g	Drain well. Dredge in rice flour if desired. Sear over medium heat until golden brown on the first side, then flip and continue to cook, or simmer in sauce, until heated through. *Fond: none*
Portobello Mushroom Caps, *stems removed*	1 or 2 caps	Sear rounded side down over medium-high heat, rolling slightly, to brown. Flip and pan-roast in a hot oven, steam, or simmer in sauce until tender and heated through. *Fond: none.*
Paneer (fresh firm cheese), *slices*	2 to 4 oz./60 to 115 g	Sear until golden brown on all sides or simmer in sauce until heated through. *Fond: none*
Cheese, *thick slices or "steaks"* (aged provolone or halloumi)	4 oz. /115 g	Sear over high or medium-high heat until browned and starting to soften. Flip and cook until warmed through. *Fond: none to light*
Vegetarian Sausages, Burgers, or Patties	3 to 6 oz./85 to 170 g	Sear over medium heat, flipping and rolling regularly, or simmer in sauce, until heated through. *Fond: varies according to type*
Polenta Cakes *½-inch/1.25 cm slices or rounds*	2 or 3 cakes	Sear over medium heat until brown, flip, and continue to cook until heated through. *Fond: none*
Potatoes, *planks or slices* (russets, sweet potatoes, or yams)	2 or 3 planks	Gradually cook over medium heat until browned on both sides and just cooked through; or pan-roast in a medium oven, or simmer in sauce. *Fond: none to light*
Tempeh (fermented soy cakes), *slices or cakes*	2 to 4 oz./60 to 115 g	If desired, simmer in water for 5 to 10 minutes to soften and freshen the tempeh. Drain well and pat dry. Shallow-fry in oil until browned and crisp on all sides and heated through. Drain well. Or simmer in sauce. *Fond: none*
Bread, *slices* (rustic breads, baguette, brioche, or challah)	1 or 2 slices	Brush with a thin layer of oil or melted butter. Pan-toast over medium heat until evenly browned and crisp. Spoon sauce over crisp toast; do not simmer toast in sauce. *Fond: none*

VEGETARIAN

INGREDIENT	Average Raw Weight (or unit) PER PERSON	BASIC SEARING TECHNIQUE
Eggplant, *planks, rounds, or wedges*	4 to 6 oz./115 to 170 g	Sear in a small amount of oil until browned on both (all) sides. Reduce the heat slightly and continue to cook, flipping often, or simmer in sauce, until tender throughout. *Fond: none (the pan may actually end up with some brown residue, but it can be quite bitter)*
Cauliflower and Broccoli, *thick planks or large flat pieces*	3 to 5 oz./85 to 140 g	Sear over medium-high heat until brown spots appear. Add water or sauce, cover the pan, and steam or simmer until just tender. *Fond: none*
Tomatoes, *medium-sized, halved*	1 or 2 halves	Sear cut side down over high or medium-high heat until the surface is charred brown and the tomatoes are just warm. Flip and plate. The tomatoes will continue to soften slightly as they rest. *Fond: medium*
Fresh Fruit, *halves, slices, or wedges (pineapple, peach, nectarine, bananas, apple)*	2 to 3 oz./60 to 85 g	Sprinkle with or dip cut sides in sugar. Cook in hot butter until browned. Flip and serve just warm, or continue to cook, or simmer in liquid or a sauce, until tender. The fruit will continue to soften slightly as it rests. *Fond: medium to dark*
Eggs	2 eggs	Panfry, sunny-side up, over, or basted. *Fond: none*

AROMATICS

INGREDIENT	Average Quantity for a 10- to 12-inch skillet	FORM
Shallots	1 to 2 tablespoons	Finely minced, chopped, or thinly sliced
Onions	1 tablespoon to ¼ cup	Finely minced, chopped, or thinly sliced
Garlic	1 to 4 cloves	Finely minced, chopped, thinly sliced, or smashed
Ginger	1 teaspoon to 1 tablespoon	Finely minced, grated, or slivered, or sliced into coins that can be removed before serving
Chiles, dried	A pinch to 2 teaspoons	Flaked, crumbled, torn, or whole (small)
Chiles, fresh	½ teaspoon to 2 tablespoons	Finely minced, chopped, slivered, or thinly sliced
Lemongrass	2 teaspoons to 2 tablespoons	Very finely minced or shaved. Segments can also be smashed with a cleaver and removed before serving.
Mirepoix (onion, carrot, celery, and sometimes garlic)	2 tablespoons to ⅓ cup	Minced or chopped
Sofrito (onion, pepper, tomato and sometimes garlic; Iberian sofrito often includes paprika)	2 tablespoons to ½ cup	Minced, chopped, or coarsely pureed
Soffrito or battuto (onion, carrot, celery, garlic, and sometimes fennel)	2 tablespoons to ½ cup	Minced, chopped, coarsely pureed, or pounded
"Cajun trinity" (onions, bell peppers, and celery)	2 tablespoons to ½ cup	Minced or chopped
Tomato paste	½ teaspoon to 1 tablespoon	As is
Whole spices (such as mustard, cumin, fennel, and caraway seeds)	¼ teaspoon to 1 tablespoon	Whole or cracked in a mortar and pestle (can be toasted first)
Ground spices (such as cumin, paprika, chile powders, and curry powders)	½ teaspoon to 1½ tablespoons	As is (these can burn quickly, so watch closely)

DEGLAZING LIQUIDS

INGREDIENT	Average Quantity for a 10- to 12-inch skillet	NOTES
Wines (dry or off-dry, preferably unoaked)	2 tablespoons to ½ cup	Deglaze and simmer until raw odor of alcohol has cooked off. Often reduced by at least half.
Vinegars (red wine, tarragon, sherry, balsamic, or unseasoned rice)	1 to 3 tablespoons	Deglaze. Often reduced and concentrated until syrupy or even nearly dry.
Stock (chicken, beef, vegetable, mushroom, or shrimp)	⅓ cup to 1½ cups	Deglaze. Can be reduced to a small fraction of the original volume for best flavor concentration, used to add volume, or thickened.
Juices (tomato, vegetable, clam, or citrus)	¼ to 1 cup	Deglaze. Some can be reduced to a syrup or glaze.
Vermouth (dry, extra-dry, or sweet)	2 to 4 tablespoons	Deglaze and simmer until raw odor of alcohol has cooked off. Often best reduced by at least half.
Sherry	2 to 4 tablespoons	Deglaze and simmer until raw odor of alcohol has cooked off. Often best reduced by at least half.
Shaoxing (Chinese cooking wine)	2 to 4 tablespoons	Deglaze and simmer until raw odor of alcohol has cooked off. Often best reduced by at least half.
Marsala (dry or sweet)	2 tablespoons to ½ cup	Deglaze and simmer until raw odor of alcohol has cooked off. Often best reduced by at least half.
Beers and ales (lager, pilsner, ale, porter, or stout—but nothing too bitter)	¼ to ½ cup	Deglaze and simmer until raw odor of alcohol has cooked off. Often best reduced by at least half.
Hard cider	¼ to ½ cup	Deglaze and simmer until raw odor of alcohol has cooked off. Often best reduced by at least half.
Sake	2 to 3 tablespoons	Deglaze and simmer briefly.
Mirin	1 to 3 tablespoons	Use as a sweetener. Deglaze, but don't worry about cooking off the alcohol.
Plum or other fruit wines	2 tablespoons to ½ cup	Deglaze and simmer until raw odor of alcohol has cooked off. Often best reduced by at least half.
Dessert wines (port, sweet sherry, or Sauternes)	2 tablespoons to ½ cup	Deglaze and simmer until raw odor of alcohol has cooked off. Can be reduced into concentrated syrups.
Liqueurs (Grand Marnier, Kirsch, Chambord, amaretto)	1 to 3 tablespoons	Use as a sweetener or finish in sweet sauces. Sometimes flambéed.

EMBELLISHMENTS

INGREDIENT	Average Quantity for a 10- to 12-inch skillet	NOTES
Anchovies (chopped fillets or paste)	½ to 2 teaspoons	Add anytime after aromatics have softened and wine or other deglazing liquid has been reduced.
Canned tomato products (sauce, puree, or diced in juice)	¼ to 1½ cups	Excellent for adding bulk and volume; add after aromatics have softened and wine or other deglazing liquid has been reduced. Can also be used to deglaze pan residues. Will thicken with concentration.
Chile sauces (Sriracha, sambal oelek, Tabasco, Cholula, or Tapatío)	¼ teaspoon to 1 tablespoon	Make sure to taste and/or be familiar with the item before you add it. Stir in anytime after aromatics are cooked and wine or other deglazing liquid has been reduced.
Coconut milk or cream	¼ to 1 cup	Add early, just after aromatics, and simmer to thicken and concentrate, or pour well-stirred milk or cream into a simmering sauce as you would add stock, cream, or regular milk.
Condiments and bottled sauces (ketchup, tomato sauce, hoisin or oyster sauce, HP or brown sauce, or steak sauce)	2 tablespoons to ½ cup	Stir in anytime after aromatics have softened and wine or other deglazing liquid has been reduced.
Cured meats, cooked (ham, prosciutto, or salami)	1 to 3 tablespoons	Chop or julienne. Cook with aromatics until browned, before liquids are added, or stir into sauce at any time.
Cured meats, uncooked (bacon, pancetta, sausage)	2 to 4 tablespoons	Chop or sliver and fry before or with aromatics. Can be drained when crisp and set aside and then stirred into the dish at the end or sprinkled over the finished dish.
Cured olives or capers	1 to 3 tablespoons	Olives can be pitted, chopped, sliced, or left whole. Added early, olives and capers soften and mellow. For more assertive flavors, add near the end of cooking.
Demi-glace concentrates or meat glazes	1 teaspoon to 1 tablespoon	Thoroughly dissolve in a small amount of hot water, stock, or warm sauce and then add to simmering sauce.

EMBELLISHMENTS

INGREDIENT	Average Quantity for a 10- to 12-inch skillet	NOTES
Dried fruits (raisins, currants, apples, apricots, or dates)	1 to 3 tablespoons	Chop, slice, or use whole, depending on the fruit. Soak in liquid to soften and plump, if you like. Can be simmered, added near the end of cooking, or used as a garnish.
Dried mushrooms	2 to 6 (will vary according to size and variety)	Rehydrate before using. Remove any tough stems. Mince, chop, slice, or leave whole. Simmer in sauce.
Dried tomatoes	1 to 3	Rehydrate or drain. Mince, chop, or slice. Add at any time.
Cheeses, hard (Parmesan, añejo, or feta)	1 tablespoon to ¼ cup	Finely grate or crumble. Add near the end of cooking or just before serving. Warm to soften, but some types will not melt. Avoid boiling.
Cheeses, semi-soft (Gruyère, Cheddar, aged Gouda, or Fontina)	2 tablespoons to ¾ cup	Grate. Add near the end of cooking and stir to melt or soften; avoid boiling.
Herbs, dried (oregano, sage, mint, marjoram, or tarragon)	½ teaspoon to 1 tablespoon	Add early to infuse the most flavor; crumble to release aroma.
Ground spices (cumin, paprika, coriander, or cinnamon, or dried mushroom powder)	¼ teaspoon to 2 teaspoons	Add anytime after aromatics have softened.
Liquid seasonings (soy, tamari, fish sauce, Worcestershire, Maggi, or amino acids	A few dashes to 2 tablespoons	Stir in anytime after deglazing.
Mustards and horseradish	1 teaspoon to 2 tablespoons	Stir in near the end of cooking.
Nut and seed butters (peanut, almond, sunflower, or tahini)	1 to 3 tablespoons	Stir with warm liquid or sauce until smooth and pourable. Add anytime after aromatics have softened and wine or other deglazing liquid has been reduced.
Pickled and preserved items (peppers, kimchee, Chinese preserved mustard, or krauts)	2 tablespoons to ⅓ cup	Drain and chop or slice; rinse if very strong or salty. Add anytime.

> continues on next page

EMBELLISHMENTS

INGREDIENT	Average Quantity for a 10- to 12-inch skillet	NOTES
Preserves and chutneys (marmalade, pepper jelly, fig jam, or mango or tomato chutney)	2 to 3 tablespoons	Add anytime after aromatics have softened and wine or other deglazing liquid has been reduced.
Peppers and chiles, *roasted or canned* (green chiles, jalapeños, roasted red peppers, pimentos, or piquillos)	1 tablespoon to ⅓ cup	Drain and mince, chop, or slice. Sauté with aromatics, or add anytime.
Saffron	A few threads to a small pinch	Soak in a tablespoon of warm water to bloom. Add to simmering sauce.
Spice and chile pastes (Thai curry, Sichuan bean, mole, gochujang, XO sauce, or minced chipotles in adobo)	2 teaspoons to 2 tablespoons	Add after aromatics have softened, or dissolve in simmering sauce.
Pestos	1 tablespoon to ¼ cup	Stir in near the end of cooking or just before serving, to keep color and flavors fresh.
Spice blends and seasoning mixes (Old Bay, Cajun, or curry powders)	2 teaspoons to 2 tablespoons	Add anytime after aromatics have softened.
Syrups and sweeteners (honey, maple syrup, agave syrup, or molasses)	1 teaspoon to 3 tablespoons	Add anytime after aromatics have softened and wine or other deglazing liquid has been reduced.
Tamarind (liquid or puree)	2 tablespoon to ½ cup	Add anytime after aromatics have softened and wine or other deglazing liquid has been reduced. Can also be used as deglazing liquid.
Tomato Paste	1 teaspoon to 1 tablespoon	Stir in after aromatics have softened but before any liquids are added, or dissolve in a small amount of warm liquid and stir into sauce anytime.
Yogurt, *plain, or sour cream*	2 tablespoons to ½ cup	Drain if necessary. Add near the end of cooking; stir well and temper by adding some warm liquid or sauce before pouring into hot skillet. Do not boil.

FRESH PRODUCE EMBELLISHMENTS

INGREDIENT	Average Quantity for a 10- to 12-inch skillet	NOTES
Herbs, *"tender"* (basil, parsley, cilantro, chives, tarragon, mint, or chervil)	1 tablespoon to ¼ cup	Chop, slice, sliver, tear, or use whole sprigs. Simmering will infuse the sauce with deeper flavors. Or add at the end of cooking for freshest aroma and color.
Herbs, *"woody"* (rosemary, thyme, bay, oregano, marjoram, winter savory, or sage)	½ teaspoon to 1 tablespoon	Mince, chop, or tear, or use whole sprigs. Add at any point after pan has been deglazed. As herbs simmer, they will soften and infuse more flavor in the sauce, but they can lose their fresh aroma. Remove whole sprigs or bay leaves before serving.
Onions and other alliums (yellow, red, white, or sweet onions; shallots; leeks; or scallion whites)	1 tablespoon to ½ cup	Add at any time as an aromatic, vegetable, texture element, or garnish.
Mushrooms (button, cremini, shiitake, chanterelles, or other wild and cultivated varieties)	¼ to 1½ cups	Mince, chop, slice, quarter, or leave whole. Sear or sauté before any liquid is added. Or stir into simmering sauce. Mushrooms have a very high water content, so do not crowd during sautéing. Cook minimally to keep them plump and juicy.
Peppers (bell, Anaheim, poblano, or piquillo)	¼ to 1 cup	Chop or slice. Roast and peel to remove tough skin, if you like. Add at any time.
Tomatoes	2 tablespoons to 1½ cups	Remove skins and seeds if they are unwelcome. Mince, grate, chop, or slice. Halve or quarter cherry or grape tomatoes. Add at any time. Sautéed or simmered tomatoes can become pulpy and thick. Add near the end of cooking to maintain a fresher texture and taste.
Chiles (jalapeño, Thai bird, Fresno, or habanero)	½ teaspoon to 2 tablespoons	Remove stems and seeds for less heat. Mince, chop, sliver, or slice. Sauté as an aromatic or stir into a simmering sauce.
Fruits and vegetables, *dense or starchy* (such as carrots, fennel, squash, corn, apples, or quince)	2 tablespoons to 1 cup	Mince, chop, dice, or slice. Sauté with aromatics before any liquid is added, or add to simmering sauce.

> *continues on next page*

FRESH PRODUCE EMBELLISHMENTS

INGREDIENT	Average Quantity for a 10- to 12-inch skillet	NOTES
Green vegetables (such as asparagus, zucchini, cabbage, broccoli, or peas)	2 tablespoons to 1 cup	Slice or chop. Add after aromatics have softened, and often before liquids are added. Blanched or precooked vegetables can be stirred into a simmering sauce. Adding raw vegetables near the end of cooking maintains firm, crisp textures and brighter colors.
Leafy greens (such as spinach, kale, arugula, or chard)	½ to 1 cup	Remove tough stems. Chop, slice, tear, or use whole leaves. Sauté briefly after aromatics have softened, or stir into simmering sauce, or add near the end of cooking to just wilt.
Fruits (stone fruits, berries, mango, pineapple, grapes, cranberries, or figs)	¼ to ¾ cup	Peel, pit, chop, dice, or slice. Sauté or soften after aromatics have softened and before liquids have been added, or simmer in sauce until softened, pulpy, or tender. Or add near the end of cooking to maintain firm textures and freshness.

ENRICHMENTS

INGREDIENT	Average Quantity for a 10- to 12-inch skillet	NOTES
Butter	1 to 4 tablespoons	Gradually add small pieces of cool/cold butter to gently simmering sauce until just liquified.
Heavy cream	1 to 4 tablespoons	Gradually stir into hot sauce. Heavy cream can be boiled, but lower-fat creams can not.
Extra-virgin olive oil	2 to 3 tablespoons	Will have the best natural flavor and aroma when minimally heated, added just before serving, or used as a finishing drizzle for a completed dish.
Nut or specialty oils (walnut, pistachio, or toasted sesame)	1 to 3 tablespoons	Will have the best natural flavor and aroma when minimally heated, added just before serving, or used as a finishing drizzle for a completed dish.
Cheeses, soft and semi-soft (Gruyère, Cheddar, Fontina, cream, or chèvre)	2 tablespoons to ½ cup	Crumble or grate. Add near the end of cooking and stir until smooth or melted; avoid boiling.
Cheeses, hard (Parmesan, aged Gouda, feta, or Cotija)	2 to 3 tablespoons	Grate. Add near or at the end of cooking. Some hard cheeses do not melt or become smooth. Avoid boiling.
Sour cream	2 tablespoons to ⅓ cup	Drain if necessary, stir well, and temper with some warm liquid before adding to hot sauce. Do not boil.
Crème fraîche	2 tablespoons to ⅓ cup	Add near or at the end of cooking. Gradually stir into sauce; can be boiled.
Yogurt (plain or Greek)	2 tablespoons to ½ cup	Add near the end of cooking; drain if necessary, stir well, and temper with some warm liquid before adding to hot sauce. Avoid boiling.

FLOURISHES AND FINISHES

INGREDIENT	Average Quantity for a 10- to 12-inch skillet	NOTES
Tender fresh herbs (parsley, cilantro, mint, chives, basil, or shiso)	1 to 3 tablespoons	Mince, chop, sliver, tear, or use whole tender sprigs. Stir into sauce before serving or scatter on top of finished dish as garnish.
Scallions	1 to 3 tablespoons	Chop, slice, or sliver. Stir into the sauce before serving or scatter on top of finished dish as garnish.
Toasted sesame or nut oils	1 teaspoon to 2 tablespoons	Drizzle over finished dish.
Chile oil	½ teaspoon to 1 tablespoon	Drizzle over finished dish.
Nuts and seeds (walnuts, pecans, pistachios, coconut, sesame seeds, or pepitas)	1 to 3 tablespoons	Use raw or toasted, chopped or left whole. Scatter over finished dish as garnish.
Cheese (Parmesan, ricotta salata, feta, aged goat, or Cotija)	1 to 3 tablespoons	Finely grate or crumble. Scatter over finished dish as garnish.
Fruits and vegetables (tomato, onion, radishes, apples, or persimmons)	2 tablespoons to ½ cup	Use raw, minced, chopped, or thinly sliced. Scatter or arrange over finished dish as garnish.
Citrus fruits (lemon, lime, or orange)	Amount varies, depending on fruit/use	Use finely grated or slivered zest, freshly squeezed juice, or wedges or suprêmes as a finishing touch.

SAUCE INDEX

Sometimes, when you are searching for dinner inspiration, it helps to turn things sideways. Here is a list of all the sauces in this book. It may help you see potential pairings with seared ingredients outside of the chapter designations.

Oils

Reductions and Glazes

Tomato and Chile Sauces

Gravies

Butters and Buttery Sauces

Cheese and Creamy Sauces

Miscellaneous Sauces

ACKNOWLEDGMENTS

First, thank you to everyone who manages to get a freshly cooked dinner to the table, even when you don't want to. You inspire me to do better whenever I feel the same.

I'm not sure how this book would have gotten done without the support of Cynthia Nims. She propped me up whenever I slumped and set me straight when things swerved. Her professional guidance is invaluable, but I treasure our friendship even more.

Sierra and Greg Boyce kept me laughing and smiling. Their enthusiasm for searing, saucing, and learning was contagious. After some elementary instructions, they ran with the techniques, creating original dishes and sharing their knowledge and skills with others. After she threw a few successful, spontaneous dinner parties Sierra sheepishly told me, "I know it's really easy, but it *seems* fancy." It's now my pan sauce mantra.

Thank you to all of my testers and tasters. You may have cooked while I watched, responded honestly while I flung platters of experimental dishes in your direction, or sent me photographs and notes of dishes you tried at home. I can't list everyone, but special mention goes to Brad and Barb Volland, Paul and Kris Latta, the extended Alki Beach crew, Chelsea Knittle, and Sophie Merrill.

I will forever be appreciative to Maria Guarnaschelli and treasure the time we spent together in the woods and "mountains" of Pennsylvania. Her vision and influence in the publishing industry is legendary. Her retirement left Goliath shoes to fill, and no one could have stepped into them as gracefully as Melanie Tortoroli. Judith Sutton remains the best copyeditor ever. Molly Stevens generously shared her wisdom and survival tips. Cameron Stauch reminded me of how magical this job is. I am eternally grateful for the friendship, generosity, and talents of Patty Wittmann and Angie Norwood Browne.

Mark Allan's perpetual optimism never ceases to amaze me. He is, and always will be, my beacon. I am trying harder not to squint.

Jeff Volland "gets me" enough to know that I often communicate better through cooking than words, so . . . dinner will be on the table soon.

GENERAL INDEX

Note: Page references in *italics* indicate photographs.

Meat. *See also* Beef; Buffalo; Lamb; Pork; Sausages; Veal
   basic searing techniques, 213–15
   cured, adding to pan sauces, 220
   temperature recommendations, 17
Meat pounder, 20–21, 87
Mint
   in Lamb Chops with Pomegranate Reduction and Spiced
      Yogurt Drizzle, 151–52
   Tamarind-Glazed Chicken Heaped with Fresh Mint and
      Cilantro, *108*, 109–10
Mirepoix, 218
Mirin
   in Crispy Tofu with 3-Ingredient Teriyaki Sauce *174*,
      175–76
   deglazing with, 219
   in Salmon with Warm Ginger Miso Vinaigrette, 44–45
Mise en place, meaning of, 27
Miso
   Salmon with Warm Ginger Miso Vinaigrette, 44–45
Mushroom(s)
   Chicken with Mixed Mushrooms and Marsala, 94–95
   dried, adding to pan sauces, 221
   fresh, adding to pan sauces, 223
   portobello, basic searing technique, 216
   Portobello Mushroom Caps with Marmite Gravy, 183–84
   Salisbury Steak with Mushroom Sauce, 143
   Seared Portobello Mushrooms, with Stroganoff Sauce,
      180–81
   Seared Scallops with Sherry Beurre Blanc, Chanterelles,
      and Sweet Corn, 71–72, *73*
   in Steak Diane, 135–36
Mustard
   adding to pan sauces, 221
   Halibut with Coarse Mustard and Rosemary Sauce
      49–50, *51*
   NY Strip Steak with Strong Mustard Gravy and Crispy
      Rye Crumbs, *132*, 133–34

Needle-nose pliers, 23
Neutral oils, 27, 208
Nonstick pans, avoiding, 19
Nut and seed butters
   adding to pan sauces, 221
   Crispy Tofu with Peanut and Red Curry Pan Sauce,
      172–73
Nut oils
   adding to pan sauces, 225, 226
   Chicken with Roasted Peanuts and Chile Oil, *98*, 99
   as cooking oil, 208
   Panfried Whole Pompano with Spiced Coconut Oil,
      61–62, *63*

Nuts
   Calamari Steaks with Garlic, Toasted Almond, and
      Thyme Sauce, 74–75
   Chicken Breast Tenderloins with Agrodolce, Pine Nuts,
      and Golden Raisins 100–101
   Chicken with Hoisin Glaze and Cashews, 93
   Chicken with Roasted Peanuts and Chile Oil, 99
   Crispy Tofu with Peanut and Red Curry Pan Sauce,
      172–73
   garnishing with, 226
   Pork Scaloppini with Bourbon-Molasses Glaze, Persim-
      mons, and Pecans, 144–45
   Seared Eggplant with Walnut and Roasted Red Pepper
      Puree, 190–91

Oil bottles, 23
Oils
   cooking, types of, *22*, 27, 208
   nut, adding to dishes, 225
   nut and seed, drizzling over finished dish, 226
   oils index, 227
   olive, adding to dishes, 225
   olive, heat tolerance of, 27
   used, discarding, 30
Olive oil
   adding to dishes, 225
   in bottles, 23
   Chicken with Olive and Anchovy Oil, 102–3
   heat tolerance of, 27
   in Salmon with Tomato, Fennel, and Saffron Oil, 42–43
   Seared Tomato Halves with Crispy Garlic Oil, 185–86, *187*
   in Skirt Steaks with Artichoke and Pickled Pepper Rel-
      ish, 125–26
   Sunny-Side Up Eggs with Turmeric Tomato Oil, *178*, 179
Olive(s)
   Chicken with Olive and Anchovy Oil 102–3
   cured, adding to pan sauces, 220
Onion(s)
   Bangers with Onion and Brown Ale Gravy 162–63
   "Campground" Trout with Sweet Onions and Bacon
      Drippings, 66–67
   fresh, adding to pan sauces, 223
   in Kielbasa with Ketchup and Curry Sauce, *160*, 161
   preparing, for pan sauces, 218
   in Seared Portobello Mushrooms with Stroganoff Sauce,
      180–81
Orange (s)
   Seared Shrimp with Amontillado Sherry and Orange
      Reduction, *68*, 69–70
   Snapper with Tomato, Green Chile, and Citrus Sauce, 52–53
   Sweet Potato Planks with Orange Maple Glaze, 193–94